Mosaic 2

Writing

4th Edition

Laurie Blass

Meredith Pike-Baky

McGraw-Hill Contemporary

McGraw-Hill/Contemporary

A Division of The **McGraw-Hill** Companies

Mosaic 2 Writing, 4th Edition

Published by McGraw-Hill/Contemporary, a business unit of The McGraw-Hill Companies, Inc., 1221 Avenue of the Americas, New York, NY 10020. Copyright © 2002, 1996, 1990, 1985 by The McGraw-Hill Companies, Inc. All rights reserved. No part of this publication may be reproduced or distributed in any form or by any means, or stored in a database or retrieval system, without the prior written consent of The McGraw-Hill Companies, Inc., including, but not limited to, in any network or other electronic storage or transmission, or broadcast for distance learning.

Some ancillaries, including electronic and print components, may not be available to customers outside the United States.

 This book is printed on recycled, acid-free paper containing 10% postconsumer waste.

1 2 3 4 5 6 7 8 9 0 QPD/QPD 0 9 8 7 6 5 4 3 2 1

ISBN 0–07–246911–0
ISBN 0–07–112393–8 (ISE)

Editorial director: *Tina B. Carver*
Series editor: *Annie Sullivan*
Developmental editor: *Nancy Jordan*
Director of marketing and sales: *Thomas P. Dare*
Project manager: *Rose Koos*
Production supervisor: *Sandy Ludovissy*
Coordinators of freelance design: *David W. Hash/Michelle Meerdink*
Interior designer: *Michael Warrell, Design Solutions*
Senior photo research coordinator: *Carrie K. Burger*
Photo research: *Pam Carley/Sound Reach*
Supplement coordinator: *Genevieve Kelley*
Compositor: *David Corona Design*
Typeface: *10.5/12 Times Roman*
Printer: *Quebecor World Dubuque, IA*

The credits section for this book begins on page 219 and is considered an extension of the copyright page.

INTERNATIONAL EDITION ISBN 0–07–112393–8
Copyright © 2002. Exclusive rights by The McGraw-Hill Companies, Inc., for manufacture and export. This book cannot be re-exported from the country to which it is sold by McGraw-Hill. The International Edition is not available in North America.

www.mhcontemporary.com/interactionsmosaic

Mosaic 2

Writing

Mosaic 2 Writing

Boost your students' academic success!

Interactions Mosaic, 4th edition is the newly revised five-level, four-skill comprehensive ESL/EFL series designed to prepare students for academic content. The themes are integrated across proficiency levels and the levels are articulated across skill strands. The series combines communicative activities with skill-building exercises to boost students' academic success.

Interactions Mosaic, 4th edition features

- updated content
- five videos of authentic news broadcasts
- expansion opportunities through the Website
- new audio programs for the listening/speaking and reading books
- an appealing fresh design
- user-friendly instructor's manuals with placement tests and chapter quizzes

Part 1 Ideas for Writing helps students generate and develop ideas for writing about topics related to the chapter theme.

Photos activate students' prior knowledge about the chapter theme.

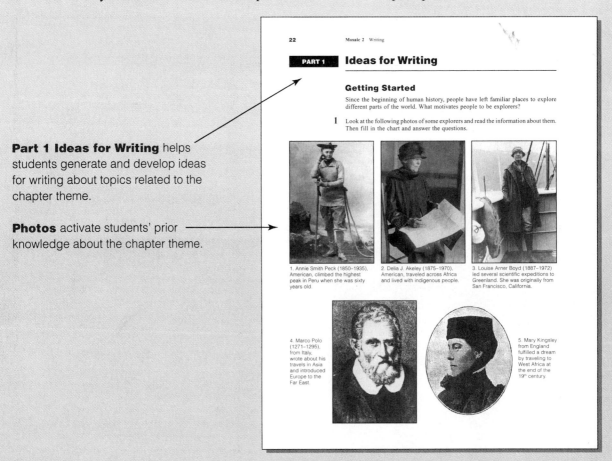

22   Mosaic 2   Writing

PART 1   **Ideas for Writing**

Getting Started

Since the beginning of human history, people have left familiar places to explore different parts of the world. What motivates people to be explorers?

1   Look at the following photos of some explorers and read the information about them. Then fill in the chart and answer the questions.

1. Annie Smith Peck (1850–1935), American, climbed the highest peak in Peru when she was sixty years old.

2. Delia J. Akeley (1875–1970), American, traveled across Africa and lived with indigenous people.

3. Louise Arner Boyd (1887–1972) led several scientific expeditions to Greenland. She was originally from San Francisco, California.

4. Marco Polo (1271–1295), from Italy, wrote about his travels in Asia and introduced Europe to the Far East.

5. Mary Kingsley from England fulfilled a dream by traveling to West Africa at the end of the 19th century.

Reading for Ideas expands students' knowledge about the theme and provides a springboard for writing.

Thinking Critically introduces higher-order thinking skills related to the reading selection.

Freewriting encourages students to explore their ideas about an aspect of the chapter theme.

Gathering Information provides students with suggestions and tools for conducting research and interviews to support their writing.

Reading for Ideas

3 The following article is from the *New York Times*. In this article, the author presents some factors to consider before you enroll in a language class. Before you read it, answer the questions.

Prereading Questions

1. In your opinion, what makes a good language learner?

_____

_____

2. What makes a good language teacher?

_____

_____

3. What's the best way to learn a foreign language? In a class? What types of books are best? How long should a language course last? What else is important?

_____

_____

Want to Learn a Language? Don't Make It a Mount Everest

It's common to see and hear foreign languages every day in New York City: rides with Creole-speaking cabdrivers, menus written half in Chinese and half in Spanish, and midnight purchases in Korean-owned delicatessens.

Learning them, on the other hand, is another matter and it almost always costs money. Finding a bargain in learning any language is rare, even though the Manhattan Yellow Pages alone list some 70 foreign language schools.

Experts in the field of foreign language teaching say become a multilinguist, you should consider several things for a language course.

Thinking Critically

Predicting

An important critical thinking skill is the ability to make predictions about the future based on what you know about the present. Make some predictions about explorers in the twenty-first century by completing the following chart. What will they do? Will they have an "urge to explore" places, new modes of communicating information, ideas, or something else? What will their work require?

Where do they come from?	What will they try to do?	What dangers will they face?

Freewriting

5 Think about the women explorers in the reading selection and the other explorers you discussed at the beginning of this chapter. What do these people have in common? What motivated them to do what they did? Money? Fame? Ambition? National loyalty? A sense of adventure? Personal pride? Write for fifteen minutes about what motivates an explorer.

Gathering Information

6 Find out more about one of the explorers introduced in this section or another explorer who interests you. As you read about the explorer, take notes and try to find answers to as many of the following questions as possible.

1. What was the explorer's background (nationality, time and culture in which he or she lived, and so on)?
2. What was his or her personality like?
3. How and why did this person become an explorer?
4. What particular types of danger did the explorer face?
5. How did he or she overcome the danger?
6. What were the explorer's achievements?

PART 2   ## Language for Writing ◄

Describing Work in a Multicultural Setting

1 The author of "Decision by Consensus" uses many words and expressions that are useful in writing about business styles. Use the following definitions and line numbers to find them in context in the article. Then write the word or expression on the lines next to its meaning.

1. a way of getting work done and/or getting others to get work done, especially in a large corporation (Line 1) = _____

2. tell others (Line 7) = _____

3. to accomplish (Line 8) = _____

4. at the higher levels (Line 11) = _____

5. political (Line 19) = _____

6. discussion (Line 28) = _____

7. persuading (Line 33) = _____

Part 2 Language for Writing presents vocabulary, expressions, and structures that students will need for writing about the chapter theme.

Part 3 Systems for Writing introduces rhetorical patterns that students will use in academic writing.

PART 3   ## Systems for Writing ◄

Types of Supporting Material

Review Point

■ A well-developed paragraph anticipates the reader's q_____ answers them.

New Points

One characteristic of a well-developed paragraph is that i_____ supporting information. There are four different types of_____ that writers commonly use to develop their ideas. These_____ statistics, and anecdotes. Note how they differ and what p_____

■ An **example** is a representative person, quality, or eve_____ common quality or illustrates a general rule. (Look fo_____ *second* sentence of the following paragraph.)

Focus on Testing

Editing for Good Organization and Development

Activity 1 asked you to read a paragraph and identify the parts necessary for good organization and development: the topic sentence, an optional bridge, supporting material, an interpretation, and a conclusion. When you have to write a paragraph or an essay in a test situation, do the same thing: Read your paragraphs and make sure all the necessary parts are included before you hand in your work.

Writing Assignments

Write an essay on one of the following topics. Use the ideas you've discussed and written about so far in this chapter as the basis of your essay.

1. Compare a rite of passage in your culture to one in the United States or Canada. What are the rites of passage in each culture? How are they similar? Different?

2. Compare the events of a rite of passage in two cultures. If appropriate, give reasons for the similarities or differences.

3. Describe and analyze a rite of passage from your culture. Give examples when appropriate.

4. Analyze the function of a particular rite or ritual. Do some research in order to cite facts or statistics or both.

5. Write about any aspect of rites of passage that interests you.

PART 4   ## Evaluating for Rewriting

Evaluating the First Draft

Step 1

Choose a partner and exchange your essays. Read your partner's first draft to get the general idea; don't focus on specific details or on grammar or punctuation. Use the following questions to evaluate each other's essays.

1. What is the main idea?

_____

_____

_____

Focus on Testing prepares students to succeed on standardized tests.

Wide choice of writing assignments allows students to select a topic that interests them.

Part 4 Evaluating for Rewriting guides students through a series of revisions that emphasize the importance of rewriting and helps students improve their work.

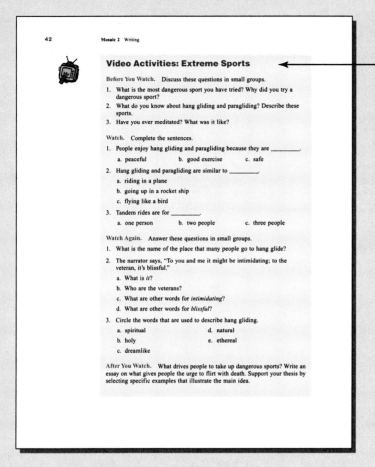

Video Activities: Extreme Sports

Before You Watch.   Discuss these questions in small groups.

1. What is the most dangerous sport you have tried? Why did you try a dangerous sport?
2. What do you know about hang gliding and paragliding? Describe these sports.
3. Have you ever meditated? What was it like?

Watch.   Complete the sentences.

1. People enjoy hang gliding and paragliding because they are _____.
   a. peaceful   b. good exercise   c. safe
2. Hang gliding and paragliding are similar to _____.
   a. riding in a plane
   b. going up in a rocket ship
   c. flying like a bird
3. Tandem rides are for _____.
   a. one person   b. two people   c. three people

Watch Again.   Answer these questions in small groups.

1. What is the name of the place that many people go to hang glide?
2. The narrator says, "To you and me it might be intimidating; to the veteran, it's blissful."
   a. What is *it*?
   b. Who are the veterans?
   c. What are other words for *intimidating*?
   d. What are other words for *blissful*?
3. Circle the words that are used to describe hang gliding.
   a. spiritual   d. natural
   b. holy   e. ethereal
   c. dreamlike

After You Watch.   What drives people to take up dangerous sports? Write an essay on what gives people the urge to flirt with death. Support your thesis by selecting specific examples that illustrate the main idea.

Authentic video clips
related to the chapter topic
provide motivating springboards
for an expansion writing assignment.

Don't forget to check out the new *Interactions Mosaic* Website at www.mhcontemporary.com/interactionsmosaic.

- ■ Traditional practice and interactive activities
- ■ Links to student and teacher resources
- ■ Cultural activities
- ■ Focus on Testing
- ■ Activities from the Website are also provided on CD-ROM

Mosaic 2 Writing

Chapter	Writing Task	Part 1: Ideas for Writing	Part 2: Language for Writing
1 Language and Learning **Page 1**	■ Writing about an aspect of language learning	■ Describing the usefulness of a second language ■ Reading a newspaper article about language classes ■ Freewriting	■ Describing foreign language learning
2 Danger and Daring **Page 21**	■ Writing about an explorer's adventures and motivation	■ Identifying explorers ■ Reading about the history of women and mountain-climbing ■ Freewriting	■ Describing explorers
3 Sex and Gender **Page 43**	■ Writing about gender differences in communication	■ Describing gender differences in communication ■ Reading an excerpt on gender differences in communication ■ Freewriting	■ Discussing communication differences
4 Mysteries Past and Present **Page 59**	■ Writing about a structure or monument from the past	■ Sharing knowledge about ancient monuments ■ Reading an article about the Giza pyramids in Egypt ■ Freewriting	■ Speculating ■ Describing ancient structures or monuments
5 Transitions **Page 79**	■ Writing about a rite of passage	■ Discussing rites of passage ■ Reading an article about rites of passage ■ Freewriting	■ Discussing rites of passage
6 The Mind **Page 97**	■ Writing about an aspect of dreaming	■ Discussing works of art on sleep and dreaming ■ Reading an article about the meaning of dreams ■ Freewriting	■ Interpreting dreams

Part 3: Systems for Writing	Part 4: Evaluating for Rewriting	Critical Thinking Skills	Test-taking Skills	Video Topics
■ Essay form and function	■ Editing for the main idea ■ Revising	■ Recognizing cultural humor	■ Editing for correct form and function	■ The School of Success
■ The thesis statement topic and angle	■ Editing for the main idea and thesis statement ■ Revising	■ Predicting	■ Planning a good thesis statement	■ Extreme Sports
■ Paragraph development	■ Editing for the main idea and paragraph development ■ Revising	■ Recognizing supporting information from experts	■ Pretending that you are the reader	■ Seeking Love
■ Types of supporting material	■ Editing for the main idea and supporting information ■ Revising	■ Using your knowledge of word parts	■ Choosing a familiar topic	■ Abduction by Aliens
■ Organizing supporting material ■ Interpreting supporting material	■ Editing for the main idea and paragraph organization ■ Revising	■ Using sources	■ Editing for good organization and development	■ College Graduation
■ Paragraph organization: levels of generality	■ Editing for the main idea and levels of generality ■ Revising	■ Interpreting symbols	■ "Drawing" your ideas	■ Social Phobia

(continued on next page)

Mosaic 2 Writing

Part 3: Systems for Writing	Part 4: Evaluating for Rewriting	Critical Thinking Skills	Test-taking Skills	Video Topics
■ Cause and effect ■ Causal chain essay organization I and II	■ Editing for the main idea and organization ■ Revising	■ Making inferences	■ Building a repertoire of organizational patterns	■ Telecommuting
■ Processes	■ Editing for the main idea and essay development ■ Revising	■ Expanding the literal meanings of words	■ Considering the audience	■ Advances in Medicine
■ Introductions and conclusions	■ Editing for the main idea and introduction/ conclusion ■ Revising	■ Applying what you've learned	■ Building a repertoire of introductions and conclusions	■ Women in Jazz
■ Definitions: Literal and stipulated	■ Editing for the main idea and definitions ■ Revising	■ Interpreting metaphors	■ Brainstorming to get started	■ A Strike
■ Making comparisons	■ Editing for the main idea, thesis statement, and organization ■ Revising	■ Making predictions	■ Getting your thesis right	■ Stealth Surgery
■ Summarizing	■ Making your own evaluation questionnaire ■ Editing and revising a questionnaire	■ Considering alternative options	■ Mastering the art of summary writing	■ Concept Cars

Chapter 1

Language and Learning

PART 1

Ideas for Writing

Getting Started

1 Look at the photos and answer the questions that follow.

1.

2.

3.

4.

1. Why is a second or foreign language important or useful for the people in each of the photos?

_____

_____

2. Can you think of other reasons to learn a second or foreign language?

   _____

   _____

3. What are some ways to learn a foreign or second language?

   _____

   _____

2 Interview a classmate about his or her language-learning experiences. Use the following questionnaire and add your own questions, if you wish.

Questionnaire

1. How many languages do you know?

   _____

   _____

   _____

   _____

2. Rate your ability in your second language(s):

   Foreign language 1: _____

   (Circle the appropriate number.)

1	2	3	4	5	6
Poor					Excellent

   Foreign language 2: _____

   (Circle the appropriate number.)

1	2	3	4	5	6
Poor					Excellent

   Foreign language 3: _____

   (Circle the appropriate number.)

1	2	3	4	5	6
Poor					Excellent

3. Think about the foreign language that you are the most fluent in. How did you learn it (for example, in school, while traveling, working, or studying in the country)?

_____

_____

_____

4. Did a teacher help you learn? How much?

_____

_____

_____

5. Could you have learned the language without a teacher? Explain.

_____

_____

_____

6. What else helped you learn this language (for example, books, tutors, classmates, the language itself was easy to learn, native speakers were helpful or friendly)?

_____

_____

_____

7. What tricks or strategies did you use while you were learning this language? Examples of trick or strategies are:
   - having conversations with strangers
   - keeping a notebook with you at all times
   - asking native speakers for help
   - making flashcards
   - watching TV with captions turned on

_____

_____

_____

Reading for Ideas

3 The following article is from the *New York Times*. In this article, the author presents some factors to consider before you enroll in a language class. Before you read it, answer the questions.

Prereading Questions

1. In your opinion, what makes a good language learner?

    _____

    _____

2. What makes a good language teacher?

    _____

    _____

3. What's the best way to learn a foreign language? In a class? What types of books are best? How long should a language course last? What else is important?

    _____

    _____

Want to Learn a Language? Don't Make It a Mount Everest

It's common to see and hear foreign languages every day in New York City: rides with Creole-speaking cabdrivers, menus written half in Chinese and half in Spanish, and midnight purchases in Korean-owned delicatessens.

Learning them, on the other hand, is another matter and it almost always
5 costs money. Finding a bargain in learning any language is rare, even though the Manhattan Yellow Pages alone list some 70 foreign language schools.

Experts in the field of foreign language teaching say that if you want to become a multilinguist, you should consider several things before you sign up for a language course.

10 *Motive*

Why do you need to learn a foreign language? Being able to order a drink on the French island of Martinique is very different from doing business in Tokyo. Or if all you want to know is how to find a telephone booth while walking near the Arc de Triomphe in Paris, a practical program in which you first learn to

15 speak, and later to read and write, would do fine.

"In this age of global travel, it is increasingly likely that students have spent time or will spend time in the country of the language that they want to learn," said Anthony Niesz, the associate director of the Yale University Language Laboratory. This means that knowing how to ask for a hotel room or for direc-

20 tions—and to understand that answer—is more important than being able to read a newspaper like *Le Monde*, or even knowing the pluperfect tense.

But if real proficiency is your goal—from being able to conjugate verbs to reading Madame Bovary in French—a university or an institute may be the best place for you.

25 *Method*

What's the best way to learn a language? Language teaching programs and methods vary. One technique is called total immersion. With total immersion, students in the classroom speak, listen to, and read only the foreign language they are learning. And for some, total immersion is the closest thing to learning

30 a language while living in the foreign country.

Since most programs emphasize dialogue in the classroom, class size is crucial. If there are more than 15 students, individuals are likely to spend too much time silent, Mr. Niesz said. The experts, however, say smaller and more expensive classes are not necessarily better.

35 For serious students who don't have a lot of time, private tutoring may be best. But groups work well for most people because they provide the opportunity to participate in games, skits, and conversation.

Teacher

What makes a good teacher? When you consider a language class, you

40 must, of course, consider the teacher. Learning a language from native speakers has its advantages, but "being a native speaker is no guarantee that a person will be a good teacher," Mr. Niesz said. He added, "By far the most important criterion is whether he or she is an enthusiastic teacher."

Phyllis Ziegler, the director of second-language programs for the New York

45 Public Schools' division of bilingual education, said that "the nonnative teacher may sometimes better understand the student's questions because he or she has also studied the target language."

So, before inquiring about the authenticity of the teacher's accent, ask about educational experience and credentials.

50 Fabio Girelli-Carasi, the director of foreign languages at New York University's School of Continuing Education, said that "the tanning-booth approach to language doesn't work." He added, "Just sitting there 10 hours won't make you darker than five." In other words, do your homework.

Postreading Questions

4 Complete the following chart with ideas from the article "Want to Learn a Language? Don't Make It a Mount Everest." On the left side, list factors that a student should consider before signing up for language courses. Give examples (from the article or from your own experience) on the right. Add anything else that you think is important at the bottom of the chart.

Factors	Examples
Be aware of your MOTIVE or PURPOSE in learning a new language.	If you're going to Mexico on vacation, you only need to learn travel phrases.

1. Do you agree with this article? Why or why not?

   _____

   _____

   _____

2. What are your motives for learning English? Complete this sentence: "I need to learn English in order to . . ." Be as specific as possible. Then share your answer with your teacher and classmates.

   _____

   _____

   _____

Freewriting

5 In your opinion, what is the best way to learn a foreign language: in a class, on your own (outside of class), or a combination of the two? Write on this topic for fifteen minutes without stopping. Give specific examples from your own experience to support your point of view.

Gathering Information

6 Find three people who speak a foreign language, and interview them about their language-learning experiences. Use the questionnaire on pages 3–4. You may want to add your own questions.

7 Share the results of your interviews with the class and discuss the following questions.

1. Was it difficult to find people who thought that they had an excellent ability in a foreign language? Explain.

   _____

   _____

2. How did most of the people that you interviewed learn their foreign language? Did they learn it in a class? On their own?

   _____

   _____

3. Which situation did most of the people feel was better for learning a foreign language?

_____

_____

4. How many people thought that a teacher was important for learning a language? How many people thought that they could have learned the language on their own?

_____

_____

5. What were the most interesting language-learning strategies of the people that you interviewed?

_____

_____

PART 2   Language for Writing

Describing Foreign Language Learning

1   The author of "Want to Learn a Language? Don't Make It a Mount Everest" uses many words and expressions that are useful in writing about language. Use the following definitions and paragraph numbers to find them in context in the article. Then write the word or expression on the lines next to its meaning.

1. the language that people from Haiti speak (Paragraph 1) = _____

_____

2. a person who speaks more than one language (Paragraph 3) = _____

_____

3. a course for learning something that you can use immediately, in a real situation (Paragraph 4) = _____

_____

4. the condition of being very good at something (Paragraph 6) = _____

_____

5. a way of learning a foreign language in which only the target language is spoken in class (Paragraph 7) = _____

_____

6. a conversation between two people (Paragraph 8) = _____

_____

7. a learning situation where there is one teacher for one student (Paragraph 9) = _____

8. a person who speaks a language as his or her first language (Paragraph 10) = _____

9. a quality or a value that you use to make a judgment (Paragraph 10) =

_____

10. the language that you want to learn (Paragraph 11) = _____

_____

11. a person who does not speak a language as his or her first language (Paragraph 11) = _____

Now add some other expressions you have read or heard for describing foreign language learning.

_____

_____

_____

_____

_____

_____

_____

_____

_____

_____

2 Write a paragraph on your reasons for learning English or another language. Use some of the words and expressions from this section or from the article in Part 1.

3   Sotirios is a foreign student in the United States. He came to the United States from Greece a year ago. When he first arrived, he spoke no English, but he quickly made lots of American friends. Now he speaks it fluently. In a paragraph, explain why he was probably successful. Use the words and expressions from the preceding activities. Remember to begin your paragraph with a topic sentence that states your main idea.

4   Maurice, a physics professor, arrived in the United States nine months ago. He studied English in an intensive program for ten weeks and then began doing research with American colleagues at a well-known university. Even after all this time, his English is not very fluent. His colleagues often misunderstand him, and he doesn't get along very well with them. Maurice spends all his free time working at the university. He never goes to any social events (parties, dinners, sports activities) with Americans. In a paragraph, explain why Maurice was probably unsuccessful in learning English. Use the words and expressions from pages 9 and 10.

5   Write a paragraph about one of the people that you interviewed for the language-learning survey on pages 3–4. Use the words and expressions from the preceding activities.

6   Rewrite your Freewriting Activity on page 8 using the words and expressions you learned in this section.

PART 3	# Systems for Writing

Essay Form and Function

Review Points

- In a paragraph, you develop and support one main idea.
- In an essay, you develop and support a thesis, which may contain more than one main idea.

New Points

- An essay usually has several paragraphs.
- The purpose of an essay is to communicate an idea or opinion about an issue and to give information to support or prove the opinion.
- In an essay, you can explain or describe something, state an opinion and support it, show the relationship between two or more things, or a combination of all of these.

An academic essay usually contains the following parts:

- *An introductory paragraph*, which introduces the essay. The purpose of this paragraph is to make the reader interested in your topic.
- *A thesis statement*, which expresses the main idea of the essay completely and concisely. A thesis statement expresses your topic as well as your "angle," your approach, to the topic. The thesis statement usually appears in the introductory paragraph.
- *Body paragraphs*, each of which develops the angle that you express in your thesis statement. These paragraphs contain specific details, examples, and facts that illustrate your angle on the topic. They also contain your interpretation or analysis of these examples. Transition words and phrases connect the ideas in these paragraphs (as well as the paragraphs themselves) to each other. These help the reader follow your ideas. In this course, you will be writing essays that have two to four body paragraphs.
- *A concluding paragraph*, which summarizes your main points and tells the reader that you have completed the essay. This paragraph is the last in the essay.

Note: Begin each paragraph in an essay with an indentation. Alternatively, you can skip a line to start a new paragraph.

1   Study the following diagram of an essay and label its parts.

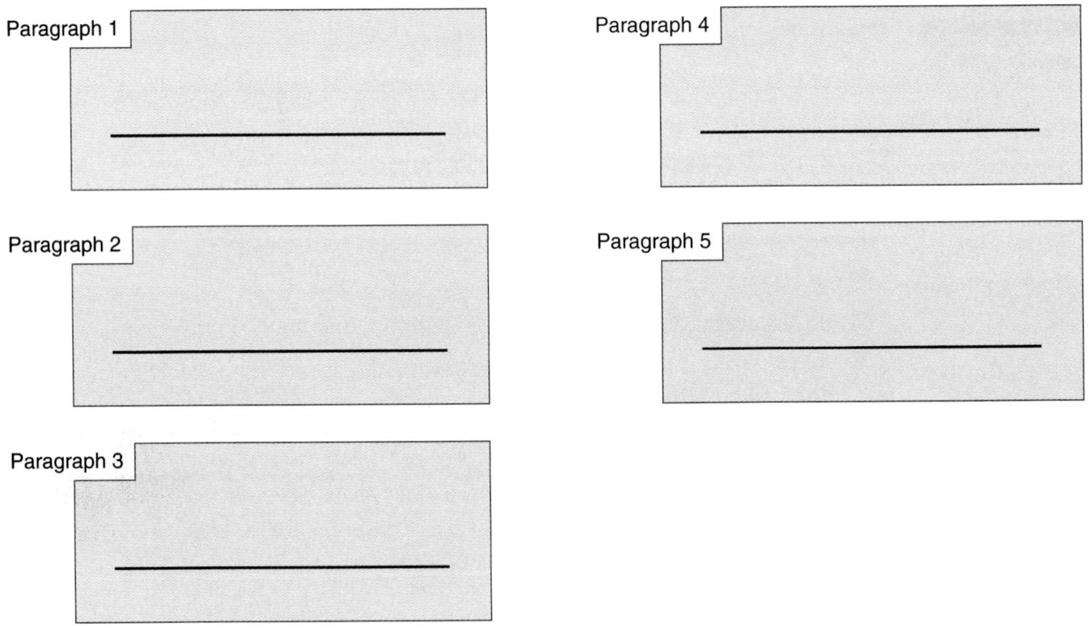

Paragraph 1

Paragraph 4

Paragraph 2

Paragraph 5

Paragraph 3

2 With a partner, read the following student essay. Then identify and label these parts:

■ The introductory paragraph
■ The thesis statement
■ The body paragraphs
■ Connecting words and phrases
■ The concluding paragraph

After you have labeled the parts, answer these questions about the essay.

1. What is the main idea of the essay?

   _____

   _____

2. What is the writer's purpose in writing this essay?

   _____ to explain something

   _____ to describe something

   _____ to state and prove one side of an argument

   _____ to show a relationship between two things

   _____ other (explain) _____

   _____ a combination of the above

3. Are there transition words within and between paragraphs? Is the essay easy to understand? Why or why not?

   _____

   _____

Student Essay: The Nature of a Realistic Person

Dreams are products of people's imaginations. They are images or ideas formed in people's minds. One characteristic that makes dreams unique from other thoughts is that dreams are, in general, projections of our inner desires and anxieties. Thus it is possible to classify an individual's character by observing his reactions and consequent behavior toward a dream. If a person's dream becomes an obsession, this person is categorized as either a dreamer or a neurotic. A neurotic's dream is a product of his or her fears and anxieties; on the other hand, a dreamer's dream is the reflection of his or her wishes and aspirations. On the contrary, a realistic person differs from a neurotic and a dreamer in that he is not obsessive about his dreams. The way in which a realistic person achieves this state of mind is by being objective, critical, and highly rational about his or her dreams.

A realistic person does not waste his time with glorious plans that will never work; instead, he focuses his energy on feasible enterprises. He recognizes when a dream is too broad or beyond his capabilities. For example, the average realistic citizen, after analyzing our present society, may imagine that all critical political issues can be solved by abolishing established institutions, such as the

Constitution of the United States. However, instead of becoming obsessed with this idea, he realizes that it is only a lunatic dream, impossible for him to carry out. For this reason, he may try to focus his efforts within the context of his dream but in a more reasonable manner. For example, he may decide to send a letter to his congressperson or join the picket line of a union strike. Thus, by narrowing his goals and focusing his attention on concrete tasks, the realistic person never ends up walking toward a mirage.

A realistic person never becomes dominated by the illusion of a dream because he or she only sets goals that can be logically achieved. In fact, rational individuals discard dreams that cannot be attained with a prudent strategy. For example, a realistic leader never leads his people into a suicidal battle to try to obtain an irrelevant victory in the name of honor and justice. Instead, he devises wise plans to utilize his people in the most efficient way possible.

The realist critically evaluates his dreams in terms of the effect that they may have on his or another's integrity. Indeed, by being sensitive, the realist avoids falling into the trap of quixotic dreams. He always considers the possible negative outcomes of his actions upon others. For example, a realist may have the fantasy of becoming a millionaire by performing a particular illegal transaction. However, he doesn't try to make it come true because it might bring dishonor and distress to his family. Therefore, a realistic person can prevent destructive impulses from occurring.

By now it should be clear why being objective, critical, and rational is what distinguishes the realist from the dreamer and the neurotic. It is also clear that being realistic is a very desirable trait. Not only that, at this point it can be stated that the realist is the ideal model of a well-balanced individual.

3   Rewrite one of the paragraphs you wrote in Part 2. Make it a four- or five-paragraph essay. Follow the diagram below as closely as possible. Then exchange papers with a classmate and answer the questions on page 13.

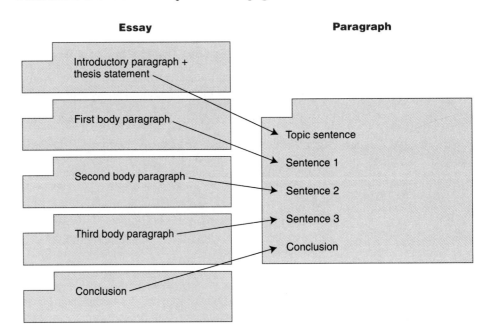

Focus on Testing

Editing for Correct Form and Function

Activity 2 asks you to identify parts of a student essay. You can follow this same procedure when you take a test. Keep the following in mind as you write an essay for a test:

- Are all the parts there?
- Is your thesis clearly expressed?
- Is your purpose clear?
- Do you have transition words within and between paragraphs? Is the essay easy to understand?

Writing Assignments

Write an essay on one of the following topics. Use the ideas that you've discussed and written about so far in this chapter.

1. What is the best way to learn a foreign language: in class, out of class, or a combination of the two? In your essay, refer to the information you gathered from your interviews.

2. Describe an effective foreign language teacher by explaining what he or she does or doesn't do.

3. Explain and then agree or disagree with the following quotation: "When a person learns a new language he (she) gains another soul."

4. Compare two or three aspects of your first language to English. You may consider:
    - Grammar
    - Pronunciation
    - Spelling
    - Writing systems (alphabets)

5. Is English an easy or difficult language to learn? Why?

6. Write about any aspect of language learning that interests you.

| PART 4 | # Evaluating for Rewriting |

In this section, you will evaluate your first and second drafts and prepare a final draft. In evaluating your second draft, you will focus on how well you have implemented specific teaching points and language use from the Part 2, Language for Writing, and Part 3, Systems for Writing, sections of the chapter.

Evaluating the First Draft

Step 1

Choose a partner and exchange your essays. Read your partner's first draft to get the general idea; don't focus on specific details or on grammar or punctuation. Use the following questions to evaluate each other's essays.

1. What is the main idea?

2. What is the writer's purpose in writing this essay?

3. Did the writer succeed in his or her purpose?

   Yes _____   No _____

4. Do you have any suggestions for improving this draft?

Step 2

Return each other's essays. Read your partner's evaluation. Discuss any questions you have with your partner.

Step 3

Now write a second draft, considering your partner's evaluation comments.

Evaluating the Second Draft

Step 1

Exchange your second drafts. Use the following questions to evaluate your partner's essay.

1. How many paragraphs are in the essay? _____

2. Does the essay contain an introduction and a conclusion?

   Yes _____   No _____

3. How many body paragraphs are there? _____

   Write the topic sentence of each body paragraph.

   _____

   _____

   _____

   _____

   _____

   _____

   _____

   _____

   _____

   _____

4. Does the essay have the format or appearance described in this chapter? Is each paragraph indented? How long are the body paragraphs? How long are the introductory and concluding paragraphs? Are the body paragraphs a little longer than the introductory and concluding paragraphs?

   _____

   _____

   _____

5. Where does the thesis statement appear?

   _____

   _____

   _____

6. Are the body paragraphs well developed? How do you know?

   _____

   _____

   _____

7. Did the writer use words and expressions from Part 2, Language for Writing, in this essay? Give some examples:

   _____

   _____

   _____

8. Did the writer use them correctly?

    Yes _____   No _____

9. Do you have any suggestions for the writer in future work?

    _____

    _____

    _____

10. What did you particularly like about this essay?

    _____

    _____

    _____

Step 2

Return your second drafts. Read your partner's evaluation. Discuss any questions you have with your partner.

Writing the Final Draft

Now write a final draft, considering your partner's comments. Turn in this draft to your teacher.

Video Activities: The School for Success

Before You Watch.   Discuss these questions in small groups.

1. Which of these things do you think are most important for students' academic success? Why?

    a. their school   b. their home life   c. their parents

2. What can parents do to help their children be more successful in school?

Watch.   Answer these questions in small groups.

1. What is the name of the school featured in the video?

    _____

2. Who takes classes at this school?

    _____

3. Which of these things does George Frasier think causes failure in schools?

    a. Children watch too much television.

    b. Schools don't have enough money.

    c. Parents are not paying enough attention to their children.

4. Circle the things that George Frasier says that parents must give their children.

    a. love   d. support

    b. attention   e. values

    c. discipline

Watch Again.   Listen for these words and say what they mean.

1. *Link* means the same as _____.

    a. connect   b. establish   c. separate

2. *Maintain* means the same as _____.

    a. begin   b. finish   c. continue

3. *Nurturing* means _____.

    a. talking to   b. taking care of   c. leaning on

4. *Structured* means _____.

    a. having rules   b. being free   c. safe

After You Watch.   Write an essay agreeing or disagreeing with the following statement:

    If a child is not doing well in school, parents should examine their home life instead of blaming the school and the teachers.

Chapter 2

Danger and Daring

You will research the life of an explorer and write about this person's adventures and motivation.

| **PART 1** | # Ideas for Writing |

Getting Started

Since the beginning of human history, people have left familiar places to explore different parts of the world. What motivates people to be explorers?

1   Look at the following photos of some explorers and read the information about them. Then fill in the chart and answer the questions.

1. Annie Smith Peck (1850–1935), American, climbed the highest peak in Peru when she was sixty years old.

2. Delia J. Akeley (1875–1970), American, traveled across Africa and lived with indigenous people.

3. Louise Arner Boyd (1887–1972) led several scientific expeditions to Greenland. She was originally from San Francisco, California.

4. Marco Polo (1271–1295), from Italy, wrote about his travels in Asia and introduced Europe to the Far East.

5. Mary Kingsley from England fulfilled a dream by traveling to West Africa at the end of the 19th century.

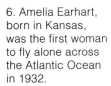

6. Amelia Earhart, born in Kansas, was the first woman to fly alone across the Atlantic Ocean in 1932.

7. Yuri Gagarin from Russia was the first person to travel in space in 1961.

8. The American Neil Armstrong walked on the moon in 1969.

9. Arlene Blum (American) climbed to the top of Nepal's Annapurna 1 (26,603 feet) with a group of women hikers in 1978.

10. Sir Edmund Hillary, a New Zealand mountain climber, and Tenzing Norkay, his Sherpa guide, reached the summit of Mount Everest (29,028 feet) in 1953.

Who Was This Explorer?	Where Was S/He From?	Where Did the Person Travel? What Did the Person Do?	When Did S/He Do It?
Annie Smith Peck	The United States	She climbed the highest peak in Peru.	She did this in 1930 when she was sixty years old.

1. Which of these explorers interests you most? Why?

   _____

   _____

2. Which explorers are you familiar with? Which did you learn about for the first time?

   _____

   _____

3. Choose two of the explorers. What dangers do you think they faced?

   _____

   _____

4. What do you think motivated these two explorers to travel to the unfamiliar places?

   _____

   _____

5. Which of the explorers in the photos do you most admire? Why?

   _____

   _____

2 In small groups, think of other explorers. These can be people who discovered new places or developed new ideas. They can be from any country and from any time period. Write their names and major achievements in the chart below.

Name   **Major Achievement**

_____   _____

_____   _____

_____   _____

_____   _____

Reading for Ideas

3 In 1978, Arlene Blum led the first all-woman expedition to the top of Annapurna 1 (26,603 feet), a mountain in Nepal. When she returned, she wrote a book about her experiences. The following selection is from Blum's book, *Annapurna: A Woman's Place.* In the section you will read, Blum gives the history of women and mountain climbing. Before you read, answer the questions.

Prereading Questions

1. What do you know about the Himalaya region? What words and images come to mind when you think about it?

   _____

   _____

2. Are there particular personality characteristics a mountain-climber must have? What are they?

   _____

   _____

3. Have you ever done any mountain climbing or gone hiking in the mountains? If so, where? Did you enjoy it? Why or why not?

   _____

   _____

4. What kind of physical condition should a mountain-climber be in? Why is physical condition important?

   _____

   _____

Annapurna: A Woman's Place

It is clear that women mountain-climbers have felt the urge to explore re-mote regions and ascend high peaks for many years. *On Top of the World: Five Women Explorers in Tibet* describes five of the many women who explored the high Himalayas between 1850 and 1920. One of them, Isabella Byrd, had been
5 sickly for most of her life in England, but she experienced a dramatic change as she traveled at high elevations in Kashmir. Unlike her experiences in En-gland, as a pioneer and traveler she laughed at fatigue, she was unafraid of danger, and she didn't worry about her next meal.

Another woman adventurer of her time was Alexandra David-Neel from
10 France. Her journeys across the high Tibetan plateau from 1911 to 1944 have been characterized as the most remarkable ever made by any explorer in Tibet, man or woman. At the age of fifty-five she disguised herself as a Tibetan beggar woman and walked two thousand miles across numerous high snowy passes to reach the forbidden city of Lhasa.

15 Fanny Bullock Workman and her husband, Dr. W. H. Workman, of Massa-chusetts, traveled and explored in the Himalayas between 1890 and 1915. They wrote six books about their adventures. Fanny, an ardent suffragette, was once photographed on a high pass in the Himalayas carrying a newspaper bearing the headline "Votes for Women."

20   Another early woman climber and a rival of Mrs. Workman was Annie S. Peck, a New England professor. She began her climbing career with an ascent of the Matterhorn when she was forty-five. In 1908, at the age of fifty-eight, she made the first ascent of Huascaran. South in the Peruvian Andes at 21,837 feet—she claimed it was the altitude record for any American. Peck described

25 herself as a "firm believer in the equality of the sexes . . . any great achievement in any line of endeavor would be an advantage to my sex" (Annie S. Peck, *High Mountain Climbing in Peru and Bolivia,* 1912).

In the years since World War II, women have made numerous significant climbs in the Andes and the Himalayas. One of the most remarkable of them was

30 the late French climber Claude Kogan. British women have also been successful climbers. From the 1950's onward, they have carried out many small, well-organized expeditions to previously unexplored regions of the Himalayas and written about them in an understated, characteristically British fashion.

In addition to the British and other small expeditions, women climbers

35 throughout the world have made significant contributions to climbing in the last hundred years. However, until quite recently women have been notably absent on the world's highest mountains. There are fourteen mountains in the world that soar above 8,000 meters (26,200 feet)—all located in the Himalayas. For many years mountaineers have wanted to figure out a way to reach their summits.

40 Attempts to climb them began in the nineteenth century; in the first half of this century hundreds of men participated in dozens of expeditions to these peaks. But even after Fanny Workman's example, only a handful of women participated in such climbs. Elizabeth Knowlton was a member of the joint German-American climb to Nanga Parbat in 1932. In 1934 Hettie Dyhrenfurth took part in an ex-

45 pedition that explored and mapped the Baltoro Glacier region of the Karakoram Himalaya; she reached the top of Queen Mary Peak (24,370 feet), which gave her the world altitude record for women for which Annie Peck and Fanny Workman had competed.

It was not until 1950 that an 8,000-meter peak was climbed by anyone. The

50 legendary ascent of Annapurna I by Maurice Herzog's French team was closely followed by successes on all 8,000-meter giants over the next fourteen years—and all by men. During this period the only attempt on an 8,000-meter peak by a woman's team was the ill-fated 1959 International Woman's Expedition to Cho Oyu in Nepal. Tragically, four climbers, including the leader, Claude Kogan, died

55 in this attempt. By 1972, when the idea for our all-woman expedition to Annapurna was originally conceived, no women from any country had yet reached the summit of an 8,000-meter peak.

Postreading Questions

4   Summarize the information from the reading selection by filling in the following chart. Skim the reading selection for details about the women explorers. Note their home countries, their achievements, and the years in which they traveled.

Who Was She?	Where Was She From?	Where Did She Travel? What Did She Do?	When Did She Do It?
Alexandra David-Neel			
Fanny Bullock Workman			
Annie S. Peck			
Claude Kogan			
Elizabeth Knowlton			
Hettie Dyhrenfurth			

1. Why was Alexandra David-Neel's journey in Tibet remarkable?

   _____

   _____

2. Fanny Bullock Workman was a suffragette. What is a "suffragette"?

   _____

   _____

3. What kind of personality characteristics do you think Mrs. Workman had?

   _____

   _____

4. What are some obstacles women climbers have faced? Do you think they still face obstacles today?

   _____

   _____

5. What interested you most about this reading selection? What would you like to know more about?

   _____

   _____

Thinking Critically

Predicting

An important critical thinking skill is the ability to make predictions about the future based on what you know about the present. Make some predictions about explorers in the twenty-first century by completing the following chart. What will they do? Will they have an "urge to explore" places, new modes of communicating information, ideas, or something else? What will their work require?

Where do they come from?	What will they try to do?	What dangers will they face?

Freewriting

5 Think about the women explorers in the reading selection and the other explorers you discussed at the beginning of this chapter. What do these people have in common? What motivated them to do what they did? Money? Fame? Ambition? National loyalty? A sense of adventure? Personal pride? Write for fifteen minutes about what motivates an explorer.

Gathering Information

6 Find out more about one of the explorers introduced in this section or another explorer who interests you. As you read about the explorer, take notes and try to find answers to as many of the following questions as possible.

1. What was the explorer's background (nationality, time and culture in which he or she lived, and so on)?
2. What was his or her personality like?
3. How and why did this person become an explorer?
4. What particular types of danger did the explorer face?
5. How did he or she overcome the danger?
6. What were the explorer's achievements?

7 Give a presentation on the explorer you researched. Try to find a picture of the person to show to the class. Prepare for your presentation by organizing information in the following list.

1. Name of explorer _____

2. Nationality _____

3. Main achievements _____

   _____

   _____

4. Dates of main achievements _____

5. Motivation to become an explorer _____

   _____

   _____

6. Challenges the explorer faced _____

   _____

   _____

7. How the challenges were overcome _____

   _____

   _____

8. The explorer's personality _____

   _____

   _____

9. Other interesting or relevant information _____

   _____

   _____

10. Your personal reaction to or opinion of this explorer _____

    _____

    _____

PART 2 — Language for Writing

Describing Explorers

1 You can use the following words and expressions to write about explorers and their adventures. Study the expressions and discuss their meanings with a partner.

Nouns	Adjectives	Verbs
pioneer	remote	ascend
adventurer	remarkable	disguised herself
rival	forbidden	figure out
endeavor	ardent	felt the urge
expeditions	notably absent	
summit	legendary	
attempt	ill-fated	
mountaineers		

2 Use the definitions and line numbers to find corresponding words in the reading selection and study how they are used.

Line 1, distant
Line 2, climb to the top
Line 7, one of the first people to do this
Line 12, hide one's identity by wearing a costume, for example
Line 14, not permitted
Line 17, strong-willed
Line 34, journeys to explore
Line 39, mountain climbers
Line 50, famous, notable

3 Choose one of the explorers you've read about in this chapter and write about this person using words and expressions from this section. Use your knowledge of the explorers, the pictures, and your imagination to make your writing interesting.

4 Write a paragraph about the explorer you did research on in Part 1. Include as many expressions from the lists in this section as you can.

5 Choose the one quality (a noun) that you think explorers must have. Write a paragraph arguing why you think this is an important quality. Provide at least one specific example to make your paragraph convincing.

6 Imagine that you are on a government committee hiring a person to travel into space to make some important discoveries. In a paragraph, describe the characteristics this person should have. Use the words and expressions from this section.

PART 3	# Systems for Writing

The Thesis Statement: Topic and Angle

Review Points

- An essay is composed of three or more paragraphs and communicates an attitude or opinion about an issue.
- The thesis statement tells the reader the main idea of the essay.
- The reader should be able to predict what the essay is about by reading the thesis statement.
- The thesis statement usually appears at the end of the introductory paragraph.

New Points

- The thesis statement usually contains two parts: the topic and the angle.
- The topic presents the general subject of the essay.
- The angle presents the writer's attitude or opinion about the topic and indicates the writer's approach to developing the essay.

Read the following thesis statement:

In the Victorian age, books by explorers were very popular because they were both entertaining and educational.

In this thesis statement, the topic is books by explorers. The writer's angle is to show why explorers' books were popular at this time. From this thesis statement, the reader can predict that the writer will develop this essay with supporting ideas to show why these books were popular.

1 For the thesis statements that follow, <u>underline</u> the topic and put a d̲a̲s̲h̲e̲d̲ line under the angle.

1. The urge to explore and discover came first from wanting to find how to live and later from wanting to find how to have fun.

2. The same motivation has driven all explorers to investigate strange new lands—this motivation comes from a thirst for adventure and a desire to know.

3. Alexander the Great was one of the world's outstanding explorers because he and his men solved many mysteries about the earth's geography and weather.

2 Look at the thesis statements in Activity 1. In the first thesis statement, the writer will discuss how people's interest in exploration came first from struggling to survive and second from searching for things to improve life. In the second thesis statement, the writer will explain how the search for knowledge and adventure has pushed people to explore. Now predict how the writer will develop an essay based on the third thesis statement.

Supporting Ideas

New Points

- The angle may include two or more supporting ideas about the topic.
- Each supporting idea should have the same degree of generality or specificity.
- Each supporting idea should have the same degree of importance in relation to the topic.
- Each supporting idea must be distinct.

The angle often includes two or more supporting ideas about the topic. The writer will generally develop these ideas in separate paragraphs. In the thesis statement about explorers' books on page 32, the supporting ideas are that these books were (1) entertaining and (2) educational.

3 Draw two lines under the supporting ideas in the three thesis statements on page 32. Each supporting idea must relate to the topic in a clear and logical way, so the writer needs to choose these ideas carefully. The following three guidelines and examples will help you choose good supporting ideas.

1. Each supporting idea should have the same **degree of generality or specificity.** That is, don't mix a more general idea with a more specific one. Compare the following two thesis statements:

   Amelia Earhart and Charles Lindbergh both made enormous contributions to aviation science.

   Amelia Earhart and the first French air-mail carriers both made enormous contributions to aviation science.

   In the first sentence, the supporting ideas are both equal: They are about two important people in aviation history. In the second sentence, the supporting ideas are not equal: Amelia Earhart is a specific person, but the first French air-mail carriers are a general group of people.

2. Each supporting idea should have the same **degree of importance** in relation to the topic. The ideas should balance: One idea should not be more important than another. Compare these thesis statements:

> Hillary's ascent of Mount Everest led to an increased understanding of geographic areas above 15,000 feet and a greater knowledge of human endurance at those altitudes.

> Hillary's ascent of Mount Everest led to an increased understanding of geographic areas above 15,000 feet and made him world famous as an explorer.

In the first sentence, both supporting ideas are of equal importance: They both explain why Hillary's ascent of Mount Everest (the topic) was an important scientific achievement. The supporting ideas in the second statement are not equally important: The first idea explains why Hillary's climb was important to science, but the second idea is about Hillary's personal fame as a result of the climb.

3. Each supporting idea must be **distinct.** That is, although both ideas are angles on the same topic, they must not be the same idea or parts of a similar idea. If your supporting ideas are too similar, you won't be able to develop separate paragraphs about them in your essay. Compare these thesis statements:

> Successful explorers throughout the ages have had two main characteristics in common: an insatiable curiosity and superhuman stamina.

> Successful explorers throughout the ages have had two main characteristics in common: superhuman stamina and incredible physical condition.

The supporting ideas in the first statement are distinct: curiosity and stamina are two different characteristics. The ideas in the second statement are not sufficiently distinct: stamina and physical condition are related characteristics.

4   The following three thesis statements need rewriting. They are thesis statements for four-paragraph essays. Study them with another classmate. Decide why they are not good, and rewrite them according to the guidelines on page 32.

> Space exploration and undersea exploration have two things in common: both are motivated by the thirst for knowledge and the desire to learn more about the world.

What's wrong?

_____

_____

Rewrite:

_____

_____

> Yuri Gagarin's single orbit of the earth on April 12, 1961, was newsworthy because the Russian cosmonaut was the first man to travel in space and the name of his spaceship was Vostok.

What's wrong?

_____

_____

Rewrite:

_____

_____

> Although Alan Shepard and Yuri Gagarin represented different countries, their early flights in space took them both to altitudes of over a hundred miles and increased our knowledge of humans' ability to live in space.

What's wrong?

_____

_____

Rewrite:

_____

_____

5   Read each of the following thesis statements. Underline the topic and circle the supporting ideas. If the thesis statement is good, circle *good*. If it is not good, circle *bad* and rewrite it according to what you learned in this section. If a thesis statement is *bad*, it may be for more than one reason.

1. Edmund Hillary proved himself a brave and courageous mountain climber in 1953 when he ascended Mount Everest.

    good   bad

    Rewrite:

    _____

    _____

2. From earliest times, humans have been driven by a desire to know the unknown and to find food.

    good   bad

    Rewrite:

    _____

    _____

3. Ferdinand Magellan and Christopher Columbus, two fifteenth-century sailors, were similar because they believed they could find a westward passage to India and because they received no support for their beliefs.

    good   bad

    Rewrite:

    _____

    _____

4. Great strides in space exploration were made in 1984, when two American astronauts floated free in space: They gathered some important information about humans' ability to live in space and returned to the spacecraft on their own.

    good   bad

    Rewrite:

    _____

    _____

5. Amelia Earhart was the first woman to fly a plane across the Atlantic.

    good   bad

    Rewrite:

    _____

    _____

6   The following are notes on topics related to exploring. Read the notes and write a good thesis statement for each set.

Jacques Cousteau
– born in France in 1910
– undersea explorer
– helped invent the aqualung, which enables people to breathe underwater
– wrote The Silent World
– perfected watertight movie cameras
– salvaged cargo from many sunken ships underwater
– made many films
– invented the bathyscaphe, which enables observation two miles below the surface of the water

Dangers in Space
– People in space are totally dependent on their vehicle.
– Meteors can tear holes in spaceships.
– Cosmic rays could be a threat.
– If people travel far from earth, certain kinds of radiation could be harmful.
– Ultraviolet rays could cause burns.

Cousteau

_____

_____

Dangers in Space

_____

_____

Focus on Testing

Planning a Good Thesis Statement

Activity 6 asks you to review a list of notes *before* writing your thesis statement. When you take a test, use prewriting techniques such as lists, diagrams, and outlines to help you compose a good thesis statement.

Writing Assignments

Write an essay on one of the following topics. Use the ideas you've discussed and the material you've written so far in this chapter as the basis of your essay.

1. What quality or qualities contribute to the survival or success of explorers? (Narrow the topic by choosing one explorer and describing the particular characteristics that contributed to his or her success.)

2. What drives people to explore? Write an essay on what gives explorers the "urge" to look for new places and ideas. Support your thesis by selecting specific examples that illustrate the main idea.

3. Compare two explorers. Highlight similarities or differences.

4. Write about an explorer. This person may be one pictured in the beginning of this chapter or may be someone who "explored" in other ways. Consider some of the following people:

Thomas Edison	Leonardo da Vinci
Albert Einstein	Ferdinand Magellan
Isaac Newton	Malcolm X
Florence Nightingale	Marie Curie
Mohandas Gandhi	Simone de Beauvoir
Wolfgang Mozart	Mother Teresa

5. Explain, agree, or disagree with the following quotation:

> The fascination with danger is at the bottom of all great passions.
>
> —*Anatole France*

6. Write an essay on any aspect of exploration that interests you.

Now evaluate your first and second drafts and prepare a final draft. Focus on how well you have implemented specific teaching points and language used from the Part 2, Language for Writing, and Part 3, Systems for Writing, sections of the chapter.

PART 4

Evaluating for Rewriting

Evaluating the First Draft

Step 1

Choose a partner and exchange your essays. Read your partner's first draft to get the general idea; don't focus on specific details or on grammar or punctuation. Use the following questions to evaluate each other's essays.

1. What is the main idea?

   _____

   _____

   _____

2. What is the writer's purpose in writing this essay?

   _____

   _____

   _____

3. Did the writer accomplish what he or she set out to do?

   Yes _____   No _____

4. Do you have any suggestions for improving this draft?

   _____

   _____

   _____

Step 2

Return each other's essays. Read your partner's evaluation. Discuss any questions you have with your partner.

Step 3

Now write a second draft, considering your partner's evaluation comments.

Evaluating the Second Draft

Step 1

Exchange your second drafts. Use the following questions to evaluate your partner's essay.

1. Look at the thesis statement. Write the topic and angle.

   Topic   _____

   Angle   _____

2. Predict how the writer will develop the essay based on the thesis statement. Write your prediction below.

   _____

   _____

   _____

3. Look at the thesis statement supporting ideas. Write them below and then answer the questions.

   Supporting idea 1   _____

   Supporting idea 2   _____

   a. Is the *level of generality* appropriate? Can each of the supporting ideas be adequately developed in one paragraph?

      Yes _____   No _____

   b. Are the supporting ideas *balanced*? Do they have the same degree of importance?

      Yes _____   No _____

   c. Are the supporting ideas *distinct*?

      Yes _____   No _____

4. Do you have any suggestions for improving the thesis statement?

   _____

   _____

   _____

5. How many words and expressions from Part 2, Language for Writing, did the writer use in this essay?

   _____

6. Were they used correctly in terms of both meaning and grammar?

   Yes _____   No _____

7. Do you have any suggestions for your partner's future work?

   _____

   _____

   _____

8. What are the strengths of your partner's essay?

   _____

   _____

   _____

Step 2

Return your second drafts. Read your partner's evaluation. Discuss any questions you have with your partner.

Writing the Final Draft

Now write a final draft, considering your partner's comments. Turn in this draft to your teacher.

Video Activities: Extreme Sports

Before You Watch.   Discuss these questions in small groups.

1. What is the most dangerous sport you have tried? Why did you try a dangerous sport?

2. What do you know about hang gliding and paragliding? Describe these sports.

3. Have you ever meditated? What was it like?

Watch.   Complete the sentences.

1. People enjoy hang gliding and paragliding because they are _____.

    a. peaceful   b. good exercise   c. safe

2. Hang gliding and paragliding are similar to _____.

    a. riding in a plane

    b. going up in a rocket ship

    c. flying like a bird

3. Tandem rides are for _____.

    a. one person   b. two people   c. three people

Watch Again.   Answer these questions in small groups.

1. What is the name of the place that many people go to hang glide?

2. The narrator says, "To you and me it might be intimidating; to the veteran, it's blissful."

    a. What is *it*?

    b. Who are the veterans?

    c. What are other words for *intimidating*?

    d. What are other words for *blissful*?

3. Circle the words that are used to describe hang gliding.

    a. spiritual   d. natural

    b. holy   e. ethereal

    c. dreamlike

After You Watch.   What drives people to take up dangerous sports? Write an essay on what gives people the urge to flirt with death. Support your thesis by selecting specific examples that illustrate the main idea.

Chapter 3

Sex and Gender

IN THIS CHAPTER

You will do research on male and female communication styles and write about gender differences in communication.

| PART 1 | # Ideas for Writing |

Getting Started

1 Look at the following photos and read the captions. Then answer the questions.

1. Man: Will you please go to the store?

2. Woman: I really need a few things from the store, but I'm so tired.

3. Man: It's a nice day.

4. Woman: It's a nice day, isn't it?

1. Are the men and women in the pairs of photos saying the same thing?

   _____

2. What is the difference between what the man in each photo is saying and what the woman in each photo is saying?

   _____

   _____

   _____

3. What is the reason for the difference, in your opinion?

   _____

   _____

   _____

   _____

 2 Get into small groups of both male and female classmates. Discuss communication difficulties that you sometimes have with the opposite sex. Try to think of the reasons for these difficulties.

Reading for Ideas

 3 The following reading selection is from a website about the differences between men and women's communication styles in English. Before you read, answer the questions in small groups.

Prereading Questions

1. Who do you think has a more direct style of communication in your first language, men or women?

2. Who do you think is more likely to do each of the following—men or women?

   - want to talk about feelings
   - use language to try to become closer to others
   - to interrupt
   - to insult others, or to not care about being insulted by others

3. When you read discussion board postings or chat on the Internet, can you usually tell if the other person is a man or woman? Why or why not?

Gender Differences in Communication

All of us have different styles of communicating with other people. Our style depends on a lot of things: where we're from, how and where we were raised, our educational background, and our age. It also can depend on our gender. Generally speaking, men and women talk differently, although there are varying
5 degrees of masculine and feminine speech characteristics in each of us. But men and women do speak in very particular ways that are associated with gender.

Some researchers describe the styles that men and women use to communicate as "debate vs. relate," "report vs. rapport," or "competitive vs.
10 cooperative" (with the first term in each pair describing men). In other words, men often seek direct solutions to problems and useful advice, whereas women tend to try to establish intimacy by discussing problems and showing concern and empathy.

Jennifer Coates, in her book *Women, Men and Language* (New York:
15 Longman Inc., 1986) studied men-only and women-only discussion groups. She found that when women talk to each other, they reveal a lot about their private lives. They also stick to one topic for a long time, let all speakers finish their sentences, and try to have everyone participate. Men, on the other hand, rarely talk about their personal relationships and feelings, but "compete to prove them-
20 selves better informed about current affairs, travel, and sports." They change topics often and try to dominate the conversation.

Dr. Lillian Glass's book *He Says, She Says: Closing the Communication Gap Between the Sexes* (The Putnam Berkeley Group) presents her findings on the many differences in the way men and women communicate, both verbally and
25 non-verbally. For example, she found, among other things, that men speak more loudly than women do, they interrupt more often than women do, and they use fewer intensifiers ("really," "much," "quite") than women. She also found that while men make more declarative statements, women make statements sound like questions by using tags ("It's a nice day, isn't it?") and question intonation
30 at the ends of statements.

What about online communication? Since gender often isn't obvious in online communication, can one determine another person's gender just by reading their written words? Susan Herring thinks so. In a 1994 talk at a panel called "Making the Net *Work*," she said that men and women have recognizably
35 different styles on the Internet. Her research showed that on Internet discussion boards, men tend to be more assertive than women are. Women, in contrast, tend to hedge (be unsure), apologize, and ask questions. Men also appeared to enjoy, or at least tolerate, "flaming" (insulting others online), whereas women disliked and avoided it.
40 In other research, Gladys We, in her graduate research paper entitled "Cross-Gender Communication in Cyberspace," discusses the results of a survey that she sent to both men and women about the importance of gender online. We discovered that most people felt that gender was relatively unimportant when they communicated online. Furthermore, We thinks that online com-
45 munication has all the misunderstandings and confusions of face-to-face communication between men and women; however, she feels that it is potentially liberating because people can be anonymous.

—Adapted from *Gender Differences in Communication* by Rose Ker

Postreading Questions

4   Answer the following questions.

1. According to the reading passage, what are some differences between face-to-face communication styles between men and women?

_____

_____

_____

2. According to the passage, what are some differences between men and women in online communication?

_____

_____

_____

3. Give an example from your own experience of each of these communication style differences: "debate vs. relate," "report vs. rapport," or "competitive vs. cooperative."

_____

_____

_____

4. What does Gladys We mean when she says that online communication "is potentially liberating?" Do you agree?

_____

_____

_____

5. What are some other communication style differences between men and women? List them here:

_____

_____

_____

_____

Thinking Critically

Recognizing Supporting Information from Experts

Writers often give examples, descriptions, and explanations from experts to support their main ideas. This helps the reader to understand the author's ideas, and it also makes them seem more valid (true) because other people have done research to prove them.

Who are the experts that the author of "Gender Differences in Communication" uses to support the idea that men and women have different communication styles? Complete the following chart with their names, their qualifications, and an example of their findings.

Name	Qualifications	Findings
Jennifer Coates		
	Wrote *He Says, She Says: Closing the Communication Gap Between the Sexes.*	
		Men are more assertive than women are on discussion boards.
Gladys We		

Freewriting

5   Think of problems that you have had communicating with the opposite sex. Describe one or more situations in which you have misunderstood or been misunderstood by a member of the opposite sex. Write for fifteen minutes without stopping.

Gathering Information

6 Collect further examples of the differences between male and female communication styles. Look for examples by watching movies, plays, or TV shows that feature male-female relationships. Look for the differences described in the article "Gender Differences in Communication," and others such as interrupting behavior, body language, word choice, conversation topic choice, boasting/bragging, or swearing. Take notes on the differences that you notice.

7 In small groups, report on the examples of male and female communication style differences that you observed in your research. If possible, illustrate the differences you found by reenacting a scene from the movie, TV show, or play that you saw.

PART 2 | # Language for Writing

Discussing Communication Differences

The passage that you read in Part 1 uses certain words and expressions to show a contrast between the communication styles of men and women. For example: *While* men make more declarative statements, women make statements sound like questions.

1 Find and underline these words and expressions in the article on page 46 and notice the way each fits grammatically in a sentence.

- while
- on the other hand
- in contrast
- whereas
- however

2   The author of "Gender Differences in Communication" uses many words and expressions that are useful in writing about men's and women's communication styles. Use the following definitions and line numbers to find them in context in the article. Then write the word or expression on the lines next to its meaning.

1. differing; changing (Line 4) = _____

2. ways of speaking (Line 5) = _____

3. related to or caused by (Line 6) = _____

4. communicate with another person (Line 9) = _____

5. having an understanding with another person; mutual understanding (Line 9) = _____

6. closeness (Line 12) = _____

7. feeling what another person feels (Line 13) = _____

8. stay with (Line 17) = _____

9. to control (Line 21) = _____

10. results of research (Line 23) = _____

11. speaking with confidence (Line 36) = _____

12. freeing (Line 47) = _____

13. unknown; invisible to others (Line 47) = _____

3   Look at the pairs of photos on page 44. In a paragraph, describe the behavior of the speakers in each pair. Use the words and expressions presented in Part 2.

4   Rewrite your Freewriting assignment from page 48. Use words and expressions presented in Part 2.

5   In a paragraph, describe the communication style differences between the male and female characters in the play, movie, or TV program from your research in Part 1. Use the words and expressions presented in Part 2.

PART 3	# Systems for Writing

Paragraph Development

Review Point

- A thesis statement previews an essay by presenting the writer's angle on the topic that he or she is writing about.

New Points

- The body paragraphs of an essay include specific facts and examples that illustrate your angle on the topic.
- A well-developed body paragraph answers all your readers' possible questions about your topic.
- You can create well-developed body paragraphs by anticipating your readers' questions as you write.

Readers usually ask questions such as:

- Why?　　　- How?　　　- In what way?

And they often think to themselves:

- Explain more fully, please.
- Give an example, please.
- Prove it!

1　Read the following well-developed paragraph and notice how the author anticipated and answered the reader's questions (in italics):

> One way in which men's and women's speech differs is in the practice of interrupting. *(In what way?)* Studies have shown that men interrupt women much more often than they do other men, while women are less likely to interrupt either men or women. *(Prove it!)* At business meetings, for example, men typically engage in "competitive turn-taking," or grabbing the floor by interrupting another speaker. *(How are women different?)* Women, however, have been conditioned from childhood to believe that interrupting is impolite. *(Explain further, please.)* Instead, they sit for hours waiting for a turn to speak, while their male colleagues wonder if they'll ever have anything to say. *(What does this mean?)* This not only demonstrates a gender difference in speaking, it also illustrates one of the reasons that men and women do not understand each other.
>
> —Georgia Dullea

With a partner, talk about the paragraph. How did the writer answer each of the reader's questions? Find the details, examples, and explanations that answer each of the questions.

2 Now read the following paragraph. It is poorly developed because the writer did not answer the questions that the reader might have. With a partner, answer the questions and rewrite the paragraph. Try to develop it more fully.

One way to learn a foreign language is to watch the nonverbal communication of the native speakers. *(Why?)*

_____

_____

Watch how people behave when they talk to each other. *(Why?)*

_____

_____

Observe the gestures they use and try to figure out what they mean. *(Give an example.)*

_____

_____

See if you can tell the difference between man-to-man, woman-to-woman, and man-to-woman speech. *(Why? What does this have to do with everything else you've said?)*

_____

_____

3 The writer of the following paragraph did not anticipate possible questions the reader might have. Read it, and in the spaces, list the questions that a reader might ask. Then rewrite the paragraph. As you rewrite, improve it by answering the questions that you listed.

Paragraph	Reader Questions
There are three areas of difference between men's and women's communication styles.	_____ _____ _____ _____
One area is using language to dominate versus using it to establish rapport.	_____ _____ _____
Another area is in the use of declarative statements versus questions.	_____ _____ _____
Using and tolerating insults reflects another area of difference.	_____ _____ _____

4   Here is another paragraph that needs more development because the writer didn't anticipate reader questions. Read it and ask questions that a reader might have after each sentence. Then turn it into a well-developed paragraph by answering those questions as you rewrite the paragraph. Use your personal experience for ideas.

Paragraph	**Reader Questions**
A good language learner has three important characteristics.	_____
First, he or she must be motivated.	_____
	_____
	_____
Second, he or she should have some language-learning aptitude (basic ability).	_____
	_____
	_____
Finally, the learner should have clear goals.	_____
	_____

5   Write a paragraph about the communication differences between males and females. As you write, record the questions a reader might ask on a separate piece of paper. Try to answer them in your paragraph. When you finish, exchange paragraphs with a partner. Evaluate your partner's paragraph by asking questions about each sentence as you read. Write down any questions that the writer did not answer. Then compare your questions with the ones that your partner wrote while he or she was working on the paragraph.

6   Select the paragraph you wrote for either Activity 4 or 5 in Part 2 on page 50. Exchange papers with a partner and evaluate each other's work. See if your partner answered reader questions as he or she wrote.

Focus on Testing

Pretending That You Are the Reader

Activity 5 asks you to write a paragraph and list possible reader questions about it on another piece of paper. Pretending you are the reader as you write is a good strategy for an essay test situation. Anticipate the questions your reader might have about each statement you write. If your statements answer all possible questions, you've got a well-developed paragraph.

Writing Assignments

Write an essay on one of the following topics. Use the ideas that you've discussed and written about so far in this chapter as the basis of your essay.

1. Discuss the communication style differences between men and women in your culture. Focus on one or more of the following:

   - directness versus indirectness
   - assertiveness versus unassertiveness
   - interrupting
   - body language
   - word choice
   - tag questions
   - loudness
   - conversation topic choice
   - boasting/bragging
   - dominating the conversation
   - swearing
   - insulting

2. Discuss the possible reasons behind the differences between men's and women's communication styles.

3. Compare the points of difference between men's and women's speech in your culture with those of another culture that you are familiar with.

4. Write about any aspect of men's and women's communication that interests you.

PART 4	# Evaluating for Rewriting

Now evaluate your first and second drafts and prepare a final draft. Focus on how well you have implemented specific teaching points and language used from the Part 2, Language for Writing, and Part 3, Systems for Writing, sections of the chapter.

Evaluating the First Draft

Step 1

Choose a partner and exchange your essays. Read your partner's first draft to get the general idea; don't focus on specific details or on grammar or punctuation. Use the following questions to evaluate each other's essays.

1.   What is the main idea?

   _____

   _____

2.   What is the writer's purpose in writing this essay?

   _____

   _____

   _____

3.   Did the writer succeed in his or her purpose?

   Yes _____   No _____

4.   Do you have any suggestions for improving this draft?

   _____

   _____

   _____

Step 2

Return each other's essays. Read your partner's evaluation. Discuss any questions you have with your partner.

Step 3

Now write a second draft, considering your partner's evaluation comments.

Evaluating the Second Draft

Step 1

Exchange your second drafts. Use the following questions to evaluate your partner's essay.

1. How many body paragraphs are there?

    _____

2. What is the main idea of each body paragraph?

    Paragraph 1   _____

    Paragraph 2   _____

    Paragraph 3   _____

3. Has the writer developed each body paragraph adequately? In other words, did he or she answer all the reader questions the main idea of each paragraph?

    Paragraph 1   Yes _____   No _____

    Paragraph 2   Yes _____   No _____

    Paragraph 3   Yes _____   No _____

    If your answer is *Yes* for any of the body paragraphs, write the sentences from each that you feel could be more fully explained.

    Paragraph 1   _____

    Paragraph 2   _____

    Paragraph 3   _____

4. Did the writer use words and expressions from Part 2, Language for Writing, in this essay? Give some examples:

    _____

    _____

    _____

5. Did the writer use them correctly?

    Yes _____   No _____

6. Do you have any suggestions for the writer in future work?

    _____

    _____

    _____

7. What did you particularly like about this essay?

    _____

    _____

    _____

Step 2

Return your second drafts. Read your partner's evaluation. Discuss any questions you have with your partner.

Writing the Final Draft

Now write a final draft, considering your partner's comments. Turn in this draft to your teacher.

Video Activities: Seeking Love

Before You Watch.   Discuss these questions in small groups.

1. What are some ways to meet people?
2. Which ways are the most effective?
3. What is the most important quality to seek in a boyfriend or a girlfriend?

Watch.   Answer these questions in small groups.

1. What does the narrator say is probably what most of us want and need the most?

    _____

2. Check the ways of finding a mate that are mentioned in this video segment.

    a. _____   using a dating service

    b. _____   placing personal advertisements

    c. _____   getting involved in activities that you enjoy

    d. _____   asking friends to help you meet someone

3. Put a check (✔) next to things that you should do and an (x) next to things that you shouldn't do on a first date.

   a. _____   Ask creative questions.

   b. _____   Dress well.

   c. _____   Be someone that you're not.

   d. _____   Ask questions to find out about your date's financial status.

Watch Again.   Circle the correct answers.

1. What does Dr. Jim Soulis say you should do before you start looking for a mate?

   a. look into yourself

   b. lose weight and buy new clothes

   c. read books about relationships

2. Dr. Jim Soulis says that the most important quality you must have to find love is _____.

   a. good looks   c. intelligence

   b. money   d. confidence

3. Which three things does Victoria Parker tell her clients to do?

   a. meditate   d. listen to a tape recorder

   b. think positively   e. become active in things they enjoy

   c. study themselves

4. Judy Knoll says that _____ personal ads are not effective.

   a. imaginative   b. negative   c. boastful

5. Men should never _____.

   a. pay for a woman's friends

   b. compliment a woman on a part of her body

   c. call a woman when they said that they would

6. Men don't like women who _____.

   a. become attached too quickly

   b. ask them a lot of questions

   c. make a lot of money

After You Watch.   Compare the information about dating in the video with dating in your life (in the past or now). What are the similarities? What are the differences? Write a short essay.

Chapter 4

Mysteries Past and Present

IN THIS CHAPTER

You will research a monument from an ancient civilization and write about a structure from the past.

| PART 1 | # Ideas for Writing |

Getting Started

There are awe-inspiring monuments in every corner of the globe: the Pyramids in Egypt, Stonehenge in England, and Machu Picchu in Peru, to name just a few. Why were these monuments built? Who built them? What do we know about them today?

1 Look at the following photographs, then answer the questions that follow.

1. The Great Pyramid of Cheops in Giza, Egypt, built between 2723 and 2563 B.C.

2. Easter Island statues, constructed around A.D. 400

3. Stonehenge, begun around 1848 B.C.

4. Great Wall of China

5. Gate of the Sun at Tiahuanaco, Bolivia

1. Locate each of these monuments on a world map.

2. What do you think is so remarkable about each of the items in the photos? Is it the actual structure or design? The period in which it was believed to be built? The location? All of these?

   _____

   _____

3. Which of the monuments or ruins in the photo interests you most? Why?

   _____

   _____

 2 Work in small groups. Have each member of your group choose a different photo from Part 1 and fill in the K column of the following chart. Write everything you already *know* about the photo. Then, in the W column, write some things you *want* to know. Leave the L column blank for now. When you have finished, share your information in the K and W columns with your group members and have them take notes on their charts.

Monument	K What You Know	W What You Want to Know	L What You Learned

Reading for Ideas

3 The following article is about the three Pyramids of Giza near Cairo, Egypt, and it describes the Cheops Pyramid, often called the Great Pyramid. Even though we don't know everything about life in ancient Egypt, scientists are able to conjecture, or make guesses, about what ancient Egyptians believed and how they lived, based on monuments such as the Pyramids. Before you read, answer the questions.

Prereading Questions

1. What does a pyramid look like? What is it made of? Do pyramids vary in size? Have you ever seen a pyramid?

_____

_____

2. What do you know about the function of a pyramid? What was its purpose in ancient times?

_____

_____

3. For whom were pyramids built? Who built them? What inspired ancient people to build pyramids?

_____

_____

4. How long do you think it took to build a pyramid? How many people were involved in the construction of a pyramid?

_____

_____

5. There are about sixty pyramids in Egypt that vary in form and present condition. Where else do pyramids exist?

_____

_____

The Giza Pyramids

The three Pyramids of Giza—Cheops, Chephren, and Mycerinus—represent the highest achievement in pyramid construction. They were constructed between 2723 and 2563 B.C. and are located on the left bank of the Nile River outside Cairo, Egypt. There is a great deal of speculation on the topic of pyramids; however, there are some well-known facts about the precise construction of the Pyramids that Egyptologists have learned from many years of research.

The significance and meaning of the construction of the Pyramids are uniquely sacred and religious. A pyramid is a huge but simple structure to commemorate a dead king. The dead king had to continue to exist in the afterlife
10 because he became divine (in part) and he had to assure the welfare and survival of his people. The most important pyramids were not constructed by hordes of humiliated slaves (as an old legend relates), but by the mass of Egyptian farmers, who were motivated to participate in something sacred. Actual construction took place only when the Nile flooded and when field work was
15 stopped. At this time the water came up to the desert and allowed the transportation of the blocks of stone almost to the place of work. It took 100,000 men twenty years to build the Cheops Pyramid, and the exceptional system of provisioning must be admired. There must have been a highly organized system for all these workers to receive the necessary water, food, materials, and tools
20 so that Cheops could be finished in time.

The immense mass of material that must have been used for the construction of the Pyramids is awesome. It has been estimated that the interior and exterior of the Cheops Pyramid are composed of about 2,300,000 separate limestone blocks, each averaging two and a half tons in weight and reaching
25 a maximum of fifteen tons. Then there were ramps that were installed and progressively heightened and lengthened to allow the transportation of the necessary material to the apex of the monument. During his campaign in Egypt, Napoleon calculated that the three Pyramids of Giza contained enough stone to build a wall, measuring ten feet in height and one foot in width, around all of
30 France. He announced this to some of his generals when they returned from climbing to the top of the pyramid; Napoleon had declined to make the ascent himself!

The building material used for the body of the pyramids was chiefly limestone found at the site, although for the casing blocks used for the exterior of
35 the pyramids, fine, white limestone from farther away was used, making maximum use of the Nile in flood. Most of the casing blocks were removed in the Middle Ages and reused as cheap building material in the Citadel and other monuments of Cairo, but there is a little remaining on the three Pyramids. The innumerable steps of the Pyramids can therefore be climbed today, particularly
40 those of Cheops, because the covering is gone. The ascent, however, is often forbidden or permitted only with a guide because the deterioration of these steps makes the climb unsafe. This is unfortunate because the summit offers an exceptional view.

In fact, the panorama from the platform at the top is one of the most striking
45 spectacles in all of Egypt: the oasis between the two deserts, the green of the cultivation in the middle of the yellow sand, the city of Cairo with its dozens of minarets, or towers, in a sort of violet vapor, the line of pyramids stretching south, the funerary temples, the small pyramids at the foot of the Great Pyramid, the Sphinx near the Arab cemetery, and the last dunes of sand beside the first
50 irrigation canals.

The view from above gives a good idea of the area and plan of the Pyramids. Cult buildings surrounded the king's tomb. There was a funerary temple on the east side, where prayers and offerings were made in chapels. These were connected by a covered walkway to a massive lower temple, which people
55 believed to be the entrance to the afterlife. It is generally thought that here purification ceremonies and mummification took place, and therefore this area was accessible only to priests.

Postreading Questions

4 Answer these questions.

1. How many years ago were the Giza Pyramids constructed? Can you think of any other structures that are as old?

   _____

   _____

2. What is an Egyptologist?

   _____

   _____

3. What was the purpose of the Giza Pyramids?

   _____

   _____

4. What was important to the ancient Egyptians based on what you've just read? What can you infer about the life and values of the people who lived during the time the Giza Pyramids were built?

   _____

   _____

5. Write the meaning of the following sentences in your words.

   There is a great deal of speculation on the topic of pyramids.

   _____

   _____

   The significance and meaning of the construction of the Pyramids are uniquely sacred and religious.

   _____

   _____

6. In your opinion, what is most interesting about the Giza Pyramids? Why?

   _____

   _____

Thinking Critically

Using Your Knowledge of Word Parts

Question 2 asks you to define *Egyptologist*. If you do not know the meaning of this word already, use your knowledge of word stems and affixes to figure out what it means. Since the suffix *-ologist* refers to a type of scientist or student, an *Egyptologist* is a person who studies Egypt. Practice using your knowledge of word parts to clarify the meanings of the following words from the reading selection.

speculation   innumerable
provisioning   deterioration
progressively   funerary

Freewriting

5 Write for fifteen minutes about what you've read about pyramids. What interests you most? What would you like to know more about?

Gathering Information

6 Choose a monument from the past and explore it further by doing some library research. You may choose to study the significance of a monument from an ancient civilization or the contemporary theories surrounding the monument. Decide what you want to explore, then begin your research by consulting the card catalogue or periodicals guide in the library. Take notes.

7 Make a presentation to your class about the research you did. Try to make the presentation interesting and easy to understand by:

- including a "catchy" introduction
- organizing your information around one main idea
- citing figures or statistics if appropriate
- telling a brief anecdote related to your topic
- including the main points of your report in a conclusion about the main idea

Be prepared to answer questions after your report and to provide bibliographic references.

PART 2 # Language for Writing

Speculating

Certain structures are used when writers are describing theories that have not yet been proven or when they are trying to guess about what is unknown based on what is known. This is called *speculation*.

1   The following speculation is from the reading on pyramids on pages 62–63. Can you locate two additional sentences that include speculations? Write them below.

1. There must have been a highly organized system for all these workers to receive the necessary water, food, materials, and tools so that Cheops could be finished in time.

2. _____

_____

3. _____

_____

One way to speculate is to use one of the modals *may* or *must*. Note the verb tenses in the following examples.

Examples

A square hole in the floor *may have been* the first stage in an unfinished project for making the room deeper.

There *must have been* a highly organized system for the workers to receive the necessary provisions.

$$\left.\begin{array}{c} \text{must} \\ \text{may} \end{array}\right\} + \left\{\begin{array}{l} \text{be} \\ \text{have been} \end{array}\right.$$

A second way to speculate is to use one of the following expressions:

$$\left.\begin{array}{l} \text{It is possible (to deduce)} \\ \text{It has been } \left\{\begin{array}{l} \text{estimated} \\ \text{concluded} \end{array}\right. \\ \text{This suggests} \\ \text{It is generally thought} \\ \text{There are many indications} \end{array}\right\} \text{that}$$

Examples

It is possible to deduce that the Giza Pyramids were built between 2723 and 2563 B.C.

It has been estimated that the interior and exterior of the Cheops Pyramid are composed of about 2,300,000 separate limestone blocks.

It is generally thought that Egyptian farmers constructed the Pyramids.

A third way to speculate in your writing is to use the adverbs *possibly* and *probably.*

Examples

Together, the three Giza Pyramids *possibly* constitute the most celebrated group of monuments in the world.

Until the ninth century, the Great Pyramid had *probably* remained structurally intact.

Describing Ancient Structures or Monuments

2 The following words are often used in descriptions of ancient structures. Write a synonym or definition, or sketch a diagram for each one. They are all nouns.

relic

ruin(s)

temple

mummy

treasure

sarcophagus

shrine

excavation

statue

tomb

3   The following sentences express theories that have not been proven. However, they are stated as if they were facts. Rewrite them by using speculations.

Example

The pyramid builders used an immense mass of material.

The pyramid builders *must have used* an immense mass of material.

1.   The first dynastic ruler of Egypt, Menes, redirected the Nile River so that early pyramids could be constructed.

_____

_____

2.   Menes and his early successors administered highly centralized political systems.

_____

_____

3.   Some of the tombs dating from the First Dynasty (3100–2686 B.C.) belonged to kings and members of the royal family.

_____

_____

4.   The king was surrounded by a large body of counselors and executives.

_____

_____

4   Based on what you learned about the Giza Pyramids, write at least five sentences describing the ancient Egyptians. Speculate about their values, their customs, and the ways in which they related to each other.

5   Choose another phenomenon from the past and write a paragraph about the people who lived during the time it was created. As in the previous activity, make inferences about their values and customs.

6   Write a paragraph about the phenomenon from the past that you researched in the Gathering Information section on page 65. Speculate about the life and values of the people who constructed it.

7   Write a paragraph explaining one of the terms from the vocabulary words in this section. Provide specific examples and sufficient explanation so that your reader is sure of the meaning by the end of the paragraph.

PART 3   Systems for Writing

Types of Supporting Material

Review Point

■ A well-developed paragraph anticipates the reader's questions and answers them.

New Points

One characteristic of a well-developed paragraph is that it includes sufficient supporting information. There are four different types of supporting material that writers commonly use to develop their ideas. These are examples, facts, statistics, and anecdotes. Note how they differ and what purpose they serve.

■ An **example** is a representative person, quality, or event. It shows a common quality or illustrates a general rule. (Look for an example in the *second* sentence of the following paragraph.)

■ A **fact** is a piece of information that is true or an event that has happened. Facts record and present evidence. (Look for a fact in the *third* and *fourth* sentences of the following paragraph.)

■ A **statistic** is a number or part of a collection of numbers that represent measurements or facts. (Look for statistics in the *eighth* sentence of the following paragraph.)

■ An **anecdote** is a short story about a person or event that illustrates or dramatizes a point. (Look for an example in the *fifth* and *sixth* sentences of the following paragraph.)

1   Read the following paragraph about Easter Island and pay attention to how the writer supports the main idea.

(1) Although modern knowledge, research techniques, and technology have helped uncover mysteries of the past, some remain unexplained. (2) The ancient mystery of Easter Island remains unsolved today. (3) The island, a tiny speck of volcanic rock, is located far away from any continent or civilization. (4) It lies in the Pacific Ocean, 2,350 miles from the coast of Chile. (5) At the beginning of the eighteenth century, the first European seafarers landed on Easter Island, and they could scarcely believe their eyes. (6) Before them lay hundreds of colossal statues scattered all over the island. (7) These massive rocks were the remains of giant sculptures that had been cut from huge, steel-hard volcanic mountains. (8) The blocks, some of which are between thirty-three and sixty-six feet high and weigh as much as fifty tons, remain today. (9) And even now scientists do not understand how such huge monuments were constructed on such a small and distant island.

—Erich von Daniken

2   Refer to the reading on the Giza Pyramids on pages 62–63 and try to locate as many different types of supporting material as you can. State whether the supporting material is an *example,* a *fact,* a *statistic,* or an *anecdote.* Record in the following chart what you find. When you finish, compare answers with a classmate.

Supporting Material from "The Giza Pyramids"	Type: Example, Fact, Statistic, or Anecdote
. . . the interior and exterior of the Cheops Pyramid are composed of about 2,300,000 separate limestone blocks . . .	statistic

It is important to know about the different types of supporting material a writer can use to develop ideas, but it is not necessary to use each type in a paragraph. In fact, as a writer, you may want to use only examples to develop your topic sentence. Or you may want to provide statistics to convince the reader of your main point. The type or types of supporting material you choose will depend on your main idea and the type of support you have available.

3 Identify the different types of supporting material in the following paragraphs. Write the number of the sentence in the appropriate column in the chart after the paragraph; some sentences may provide more than one type of supporting material. Ignore sentences that are not numbered.

a. (1) Stonehenge, in Wiltshire, England, is an ancient monument that still mystifies scientists. (2) It is a group of huge rough-cut stones that probably marks the site of an ancient religious structure. (3) The monument dates from about 1848 B.C. and was originally a circular arrangement of blocks of gray sandstone, each about thirty feet long and weighing an average of twenty-eight tons. (4) There were three sets of stones inside this hundred-foot circle, and near the center was a sixteen-foot block of flat sandstone, which was probably an altar. Although scientists have been able to approximate the age of the monument, they can only conjecture about why the huge stones were transported there. No one knows exactly who brought them.

Example	Fact	Statistic	Anecdote

b. (1) One of the great archaeological wonders of South America is the monolithic Gate of the Sun at Tiahuanaco. (2) It is a gigantic sculpture, nearly ten feet high and sixteen and a half feet wide, carved out of a single block. (3) The weight of this piece of masonry is estimated to be more than ten tons. Pictured on the rock are forty-eight square figures in three rows next to a flying god. Legend tells of a golden "spaceship" that came to this city from the stars. (6) In the spaceship came a woman, Oryana, who had four webbed fingers and who was to become the Great Mother of the earth. After giving birth to seventy earth children, Oryana returned to the stars. (8) One does, in fact, find rock drawings of beings with four fingers within the city. But their ages cannot be determined. There is no plausible explanation for the beginning or end of civilization in this city or for the great Gate of the Sun.

Example	Fact	Statistic	Anecdote

4   Antipater of Sidon compiled a list of the seven wonders of his time in the second century B.C. These are listed below with brief descriptive notes. Choose two of these wonders and write a paragraph about each of them. You may have to gather more information in order to include enough support to fully develop your topic sentences.

Giza Pyramids

- Tombs of Egyptian kings
- Only ancient wonder still standing
- Took 100,000 people 20 years to build

Statue of Zeus at Olympia

- Seemed like a living god to ancient Greeks
- Carved by Phidias for original Olympics
- Fifth century B.C.
- 40 feet high
- Contained ivory, gold, precious stones
- Showed Zeus on his throne

Mausoleum at Halicarnassus

- Built by Queen Artemisia in Asia Minor for her husband, King Mausolus, who died in 353 B.C.
- He was known as a wise king
- Statues and carvings told of his reign
- The word *mausoleum* originated from this structure

Pharos of Alexandria

- Lighthouse built around 240 B.C.
- 400 feet high
- Helped seafarers for 1,500 years

Hanging Gardens of Babylon

- Living green miracle in a desert city
- Built by King Nebuchadnezzar for his wife
- A series of terraces with flowers, shrubs, and trees

Temple of Diana at Ephesus

- Built of marble
- More than 400 feet long
- Had more than 100 columns, 60 feet high
- Took 120 years to build

Colossus of Rhodes

- Gigantic statue of Helios, the sun god
- In harbor on island of Rhodes
- Third century B.C.
- The word *colossal* comes from this statue
- 105 feet tall

5   Choose one of the following natural wonders and write a paragraph about it. You may want to do some research to gather supporting information.

Mount Everest, 29,028 feet high, on Nepal-Tibet border

Victoria Falls, on the Zambezi River in Zimbabwe

Grand Canyon, Colorado River, Arizona

Great Barrier Reef of Australia, world's largest coral formation

Caves of Altamira, or other caves in France or Spain with prehistoric paintings

Paricutín, a volcano in Mexico

The harbor in Rio de Janeiro, Brazil

Focus on Testing

Choosing a Familiar Topic

Activities 4 and 5 ask you to make a choice about what you will write. When you are given a choice, choose a topic that is familiar to you. You will write faster and with more confidence if you write about something you already know.

Writing Assignments

Write an essay on one of the following topics. Use the ideas you've discussed and the material you've written so far in this chapter as the basis of your essay.

1. Choose an ancient structure or a mysterious phenomenon from the past that interests you. Speculate on its purpose and the methods used to build it, including any theories you know of to explain it.

2. Compare structures of the past that were constructed at about the same time or for the same purpose.

3. Develop one of the activities from a previous section into an essay. Choose an activity that you spent time on and that interested you. Clarify the purpose of your essay and formulate a preliminary thesis statement to get you started.

4. Write an essay about any topic related to past mysteries that interests you.

| PART 4 | # Evaluating for Rewriting |

Evaluating the First Draft

Step 1

Choose a partner and exchange your essays. Read your partner's first draft to get the general idea; don't focus on specific details or on grammar or punctuation. Use the following questions to evaluate each other's essays.

1. What is the main idea?

   _____

   _____

2. What is the writer's purpose in writing this essay?

   _____

   _____ : _____

3. Did the writer accomplish what he or she set out to do?

   Yes _____   No _____

4. Do you have any suggestions for improving this draft?

   _____

   _____

Step 2

Return each other's essays. Read your partner's evaluation. Discuss any questions you have with your partner.

Step 3

Now write a second draft, considering your partner's evaluation comments.

Evaluating the Second Draft

Step 1

Exchange your second drafts. Use the following questions to evaluate your partner's essay.

1. Based on the thesis statement, how do you expect the writer to develop this essay? List the types of supporting material you expect to find.

   _____

   _____

2. Read all the body paragraphs and answer the following questions for each one.

   Paragraph 1

   How many types of supporting material are used? _____

   Identify each type and give an example.

   _____

   _____

   Could the writer add a different or additional type of supporting material to develop the paragraph further?

   _____

   _____

   Paragraph 2

   How many types of supporting material are used? _____

   Identify each type and give an example.

   _____

   _____

   Could the writer add a different or additional type of supporting material to develop the paragraph further?

   _____

   _____

Paragraph 3

How many types of supporting material are used? _____

Identify each type and give an example.

_____

_____

Could the writer add a different or additional type of supporting material to develop the paragraph further?

_____

_____

3. How many words and expressions from Part 2, Language for Writing, did the writer use in this essay?

_____

4. Were they used correctly in terms of both meaning and grammar?

Yes _____   No _____

5. Do you have any suggestions for the writer in future work?

_____

_____

6. What are the strengths of this essay?

_____

_____

Step 2

Return your second drafts. Read your partner's evaluation. Discuss any questions you have with your partner.

Writing the Final Draft

Now write a final draft, considering your partner's comments. Turn in this draft to your teacher.

Video Activities: Abduction by Aliens

Before You Watch.   Discuss these questions in small groups.

1. Do you think that people from other planets have visited Earth? Have you ever seen a UFO? (Unidentified Flying Object)

    Abduct means the same as _____.

    a. borrow   b. kidnap   c. visit

Watch.   Answer these questions in small group.

1. Ruth Foley says that she _____.

    a. has been abducted by people from outer space

    b. was born in outer space

    c. has visited other planets

2. What do the abductors look like? Write a description.

    _____

    _____

    _____

3. According to Ruth, what is the abductors' purpose?

    a. to perform medical tests

    b. to ask people about life on Earth

    c. to tell people about their planet

4. People in Indiana say that _____ burned the ground near a house in Indiana.

    a. an abductor   b. a light   c. a spaceship

5. The author of *Secret Life* _____ abductions really happen.

    a. isn't sure if   b. is positive that   c. doesn't believe that

Watch Again.   Write answers to these questions.

1. How old was Ruth Foley when she was first abducted?

    _____

2. Who once saw Ruth being abducted?

    _____

3. What was the year of the abduction in Indiana?

    _____

4. How long did it take for the grass to grow on the burned spot?

_____

5. Who is John Mack and what did he write?

_____

_____

6. What does John Mack believe?

_____

_____

After You Watch.   Write an essay explaining why you believe or do not believe in UFOs and abduction stories such as Ruth Foley's. Support your opinion with examples from the video and other information you may have about this subject.

Chapter 5

Transitions

PART 1	# Ideas for Writing

Getting Started

1   Look at the photos. They illustrate some North American *rites of passage* (ceremonies, rituals, or events that mark important changes, or transitions, in a person's life). Read the captions; they explain the meanings of the rites of passage in American culture. Then answer the questions that follow.

1. Starting school (age 5–6). The child's focus changes from inside the home to outside the home.

2. Obtaining a driver's license (age 16–18). Being able to drive alone results in greater independence.

3. Graduating from secondary school (age 17–18). At this age, people have a choice between work or further education. This also often involves moving away from home.

4. Graduating from college or university (age 21–22). Childhood is over; people usually become financially independent by this age.

5. Getting married. Responsibility extends to another person.

6. Having children. Financial responsibilities increase.

7. Retiring. The freedom to structure time as one chooses can be pleasurable or problematic.

1. The first two photos show events in which people gain independence. Can you explain how?

2. Do the other events mark points at which people gain or lose independence? Explain your answer.

2   Think about rites of passage in a culture you are familiar with. What do they mean? Complete the following chart.

Country/Culture: _____

Event	Age	Meaning

3   Compare your chart with the photos illustrating North American rites of passage. Discuss the differences with your classmates.

Reading for Ideas

4   The following article comes from a college sociology textbook. The two American authors are describing rites of passage in their own culture. Before you read, answer the questions in small groups.

Prereading Questions

1.   What does *adolescence* mean? What is another word for an *adolescent*?

_____

_____

2.   Look at the photos on pages 80–81 and your chart on page 82. Which events indicate that a person has become an adult?

_____

_____

3.   Discuss the lives of adolescents in your culture. What do they do in their free time? Are they close to their families? Are they independent?

_____

_____

4.   Discuss the lives, responsibilities, attitudes, and thoughts of the middle-aged people that you know in your culture. Do they fear growing old? Are they sometimes disappointed in how their lives turned out?

_____

_____

Rites of Passage in American Society

In some cultures, people mark stages of development with specific ceremonies. Many societies have definite rites of passage that dramatize and validate changes in a person's status (position or place in a society). For example, a young Aboriginal woman in Australia will be honored at a ceremony at the first
5   sign of physical maturity. During these festivities, her first, unborn daughter is betrothed to a grown man. This is the source of the Aboriginal expression "There is no such thing as an unmarried woman" (Goodale, 1971). For the Aborigines, there is a sharp dividing line between childhood and the responsibilities of adult life.
10   This is not the case in American culture; however, several psychologists and sociologists have given particular labels to various periods of socialization. In the United States, people do not necessarily move from one stage to another in the clear-cut way that they are promoted from one grade in school to another. This may lead to some ambiguity and confusion as we grow up: At a certain age

15 and level of maturity, are we children or adolescents? At another, are we adolescents or adults? In fact, studies show that there is increasing disagreement
among middle-aged, middle class Americans about the appropriate age for
certain life events.

   American society is somewhat
20 similar to simpler societies such as
that of the Aborigines in that we have
events that indicate when we acquire
new roles and statuses. The wedding
represents a rite of passage for
25 Americans; yet, there is no one ceremony that clearly marks the transition from childhood to adulthood.
Instead, we go through a prolonged
period of transition known as adoles-
30 cence. This transition varies depending on certain social factors,
especially social class. For example,
a person from a poor background
may not have any alternatives but to
35 work full time at a rather early age.
Because he or she may need to contribute to the family income or to become financially self-supporting,
such a young person may not be able
40 to attend college, and therefore delay going to work.

   Even after he or she becomes an adult, an American will still pass through
a series of developmental stages. Psychologist Daniel Levinson (1978) studied
American males and identified three major transitional periods that occur during
45 men's lifetimes. One of these begins at about age 40. American men often
experience a stressful period of self-evaluation, commonly known as the midlife
crisis. In this period, men may realize that they have not achieved basic goals
and ambitions and that they do not have much time left to do so. Levinson
(1978:199) found that 80 percent of the men that he surveyed experienced
50 these tumultuous midlife conflicts.

   While his conclusions are also true for many women—especially those who
follow similar career patterns to men—they do not necessarily apply to women.
A key aspect of Levinson's work is the idea that, when young, men have a dream
of what the adult world is like—a vision that creates excitement and a sense of
55 possibility. However, until recently, most women were socialized into becoming
wives and mothers instead of entering the paid work force. Moreover, most
women carry the role of "mother" throughout their lives; society sees this role as
more time-consuming and more important than the role of "father" for men.

   Some researchers, however, state that the midlife crisis is clearly evident
60 in both sexes. In her book *Pathfinders*, Gail Sheehy (1981:63) found that American women experience fear and confusion in their midlife years when they see
the gaps between their youthful hopes and ideas and their present lives.
Sheehy's studies suggest that midlife turmoil may begin somewhat earlier for
women than for men, often at about age 35. Women typically outlive males of
65 the same age, including their husbands; this is an important factor in the midlife

crises of American women. Consequently, as she reaches midlife, a woman faces a future in which she may eventually live alone and may become dependent on her children (Baruchetal, 1983:238–241; Rosenfeld and Stark, 1987:64, 66).

70   Is the midlife crisis unique to the United States? In some cultures, people are given specific goals during childhood that they are able to achieve early in life. However, in American society, people have a great deal of freedom to choose their own goals. This has an unintended consequence: it leaves a great deal of room for indecision or even failure.

75   Levinson identified a final period of transition, the late-adult transition, which occurs between 60 and 65 years of age. At this time, many Americans begin working less and prepare for retirement. However, it is important to note that the nation's attitudes toward aging have undergone a dramatic change in recent decades. No longer is it widely accepted that older people should simply sit
80 around doing nothing but wait to die. Instead, there has been an increase in programs to socialize the elderly for meaningful activities.

—Adapted from *Sociology*, Fourth Edition, by Richard T. Schaefer and Robert P. Lamm

Postreading Questions

5 Answer these questions.

1. According to the passage, is there a clear difference between childhood and adulthood in American culture? Give an example of a culture that clearly marks the difference between childhood and adulthood.

_____

_____

2. Explain how the length of adolescence might differ within American culture.

_____

_____

3. Describe a transition that many American adults, especially men, experience. How might this transition be the same or different for American women?

_____

_____

4. How have attitudes toward aging changed in American culture in recent years?

_____

_____

5. How common is the midlife crisis in a culture you are familiar with? What is the role of older people in this culture?

_____

_____

Thinking Critically

Using Sources

In academic writing, it is important to indicate the source of facts and other information that the writer uses to support his or her ideas. You may have noticed in the textbook passage that you just read names and dates in parentheses after certain statements, for example:

Consequently, as she reaches midlife, a woman faces a future in which she may eventually live alone and may become dependent on her children (Baruchetal, 1983:238–241; Rosenfeld and Stark, 1987:64, 66).

The information in parentheses means that several researchers—Baruchetal, Rosenfeld, and Stark—all discovered this information about women in midlife, and each reported it in papers that they published. The years refer to the publication dates of their papers; the numbers after the colons indicate the pages in the journals on which they reported this information.

Textbook authors cite these sources so readers know where the ideas come from, and so that they can look them up themselves, if they want to.

Try this yourself: find the 1981 edition of the Gail Sheehy book, *Pathfinders*, in a library. See if you can find the source of the fact that "American women experience fear and confusion in their midlife years as they see the gaps between their youthful hopes and ideas and their present lives."

Freewriting

6 Choose a rite of passage from a culture you are familiar with and write about it for fifteen minutes without stopping. Include as much information as you can about how a person changes after this event and how others regard her or him before and after this passage. Refer to the chart you completed on rites of passage on page 82.

Gathering Information

7 Collect information on a rite of passage from a culture that interests you by interviewing someone from that culture. You may consider religious and ethnic rites of passage—for example, confirmation, bar or bat mitzvah, or quinceaños. Before the interview, think of what you would like to know and add questions to the following, if necessary.

Name: _____

Sex: _____

Age: _____

Rite of passage: _____

What does the rite of passage involve (What happens?)

_____

_____

What is the person's status before the rite?

_____

_____

What is the person's status after the rite?

_____

_____

What is the history of the rite in this culture? Why or how has it become an important event?

_____

_____

_____

_____

_____

_____

_____

Additional information/comments:

_____

_____

8   Give a brief presentation on the rite of passage that you learned about. If possible, bring pictures, photos, music, or objects associated with the rite to make your presentation more interesting.

PART 2   # Language for Writing

Discussing Rites of Passage

1   The author of "Rites of Passage in American Society" uses many words and expressions that are useful in writing about transitions. Use the following definitions and line numbers to find them in context in the article. Then write the word or expression on the lines next to its meaning.

1. having the body of an adult (Line 5) = _____

2. celebrations or special events (Line 5) = _____

3. promised to marry (Line 6) = _____

4. the process of teaching someone to behave according to a group's rules or values (Line 11) = _____

5. the state of being unclear (Line 14) = _____

6. made longer (Line 28) = _____

7. a time of difficulty (Line 47) = _____

8. upsetting (Line 50) = _____

9. confusion (Line 63) = _____

10. to live longer than (Line 64) = _____

2   Some words that are useful in writing about transitions have many forms. Study the forms of these words from the reading. Add any other that you noticed.

Nouns	Verbs	Adjectives
maturity	mature	mature
adolescence		adolescent
socialization	socialize	socialized
transition		transitional
retirement	retire	retired
_____	_____	_____
_____	_____	_____
_____	_____	_____

3 Write a paragraph about the rite of passage that you learned about from the interview on page 87 in Part 1. Use as many of the words and expressions from this section as you can.

4 Rewrite your Freewriting assignment from page 86, Part 1, using words and expressions presented in this section.

5 Write a paragraph about adolescence, midlife, or late adulthood in your culture. Concentrate on the changes that a person makes during this period, and use words and expressions from this section.

PART 3 # Systems for Writing

Organizing Supporting Material

Review Points
■ You can use different kinds of supporting information to develop the main ideas of a paragraph: examples, facts, statistics, and anecdotes.
■ You can use different types of support in one paragraph, or use the same kind.
■ The type of support you choose depends on the main idea of your paragraph.

New Points
■ A well-developed paragraph includes the following: a topic sentence, an optional bridge statement, supporting material, and a conclusion.
■ These parts of a well-developed paragraph have the following purposes:
1. The *topic sentence* expresses the main idea.
2. The *bridge* explains the main idea and connects it to the supporting material.
3. The *supporting material* includes examples, facts, statistics, or an anecdote.
4. The *conclusion* reminds the reader of the main idea and concludes the paragraph.

1 Read the following paragraph and identify its parts (topic sentence, bridge, supporting material, and conclusion) by answering the questions.

---

(1) Adolescents form a large and powerful group in American society. (2) Teenagers, as they are called in the United States and Canada, receive a lot of attention because of their purchasing power. (3) They are important targets for advertisers of clothing companies, which introduce many fashions designed especially for teen taste and lifestyle. (4) Special magazines, books, and newspaper columns are also written only for teens. (5) The entertainment industry has a huge market in its vast audience of teenagers. (6) Finally, a variety of products are designed exclusively for young Americans between twelve and twenty. (7) Indeed, adolescents in America receive a lot of attention and form a powerful group.

What is Sentence 1? _____

What is Sentence 2? _____

What is Sentence 3? _____

What is Sentence 4? _____

What is Sentence 5? _____

What is Sentence 6? _____

What is Sentence 7? _____

Interpreting Supporting Material

New Points

■ A well-developed paragraph often includes an interpretation (or analysis) of the supporting material.

■ An interpretation is one or more sentences that follow the supporting material. It explains how the supporting material relates to and develops the topic sentence.

2 Read the following paragraph and notice how the interpretation (underlined) connects the supporting material and the topic sentence.

Topic sentence	At age six, a child begins to separate himself from his family and to take his place as a responsible citizen of the
Bridge	outside world. This act of separating includes many changes
Example 1	in behavior and attitude. He becomes more independent of
Example 2	his parents and often can get impatient with them. He is more
Example 3	concerned with what other children say and do. He becomes interested in impersonal subjects like arithmetic and engines.
Interpretation	<u>The change in interest from parents and personal subjects to peers and less personal subjects is a clear indication of this movement toward independence.</u> It is at six, then, that the path to self-sufficiency and adulthood begins.

3 Read the following paragraphs and identify the parts by labeling each sentence, as you saw in the previous paragraph.

_____ For many Americans, high school graduation marks the beginning of adulthood. It is at this time that young people assume adult responsibilities. For example, they move away from home after high school, and have their own domestic concerns. Also, they are often partly if not fully responsible for supporting themselves financially. Finally, they are expected to make their own decisions. Thus, the assumption of both personal and financial responsibilities is the true initiation into adulthood. So it is at the end of high school that Americans become adults.

_____ The transition from middle to old age is a period of critical biological and social change for the male. Physical decline disrupts habitual activity, and retirement changes one's lifestyle dramatically. Because of the changes in social role, retirement can also bring feelings of uselessness. These changes can cause a person to feel alienated and alone. It is important to be aware of the highly sensitive transition from middle to old age.

4   Complete the following topic sentence and bridge sentence and think of some supporting examples for your topic sentence. Then use your topic sentence, bridge sentence, and supporting information to write a complete paragraph by adding supporting material, an interpretation, and a conclusion. Use the paragraph in Activity 1 on page 90 as a model.

- Topic sentence: For someone from my culture, the transition from

  adolescence to adulthood can occur _____

  _____ (time or age).

- Bridge sentence: This is due to _____

  _____ (reason the transition

  happens at this time or age).

- Supporting examples:

  _____

  _____

  _____

- Interpretation:

  _____

  _____

  _____

  _____

- Conclusion:

  _____

  _____

5   Write a paragraph using the following topic sentence:

Starting school is an important step for children in any culture because it marks their first break with home.

6   Write a paragraph about a personal or social transition. Use all of the parts of a well-developed paragraph that you reviewed in this section.

7   Exchange one or more paragraphs from the activities you did on page 89, Part 2, with a partner. Check to see if your partner has used all of the parts of a well-organized and developed paragraph. Rewrite the material if necessary.

Focus on Testing

Editing for Good Organization and Development

Activity 1 asked you to read a paragraph and identify the parts necessary for good organization and development: the topic sentence, an optional bridge, supporting material, an interpretation, and a conclusion. When you have to write a paragraph or an essay in a test situation, do the same thing: Read your paragraphs and make sure all the necessary parts are included before you hand in your work.

Writing Assignments

Write an essay on one of the following topics. Use the ideas you've discussed and written about so far in this chapter as the basis of your essay.

1. Compare a rite of passage in your culture to one in the United States or Canada. What are the rites of passage in each culture? How are they similar? Different?

2. Compare the events of a rite of passage in two cultures. If appropriate, give reasons for the similarities or differences.

3. Describe and analyze a rite of passage from your culture. Give examples when appropriate.

4. Analyze the function of a particular rite or ritual. Do some research in order to cite facts or statistics or both.

5. Write about any aspect of rites of passage that interests you.

PART 4 # Evaluating for Rewriting

Evaluating the First Draft

Step 1

Choose a partner and exchange your essays. Read your partner's first draft to get the general idea; don't focus on specific details or on grammar or punctuation. Use the following questions to evaluate each other's essays.

1. What is the main idea?

_____

_____

_____

2. What is the writer's purpose in writing this essay?

    _____

    _____

    _____

3. Did the writer accomplish what he or she set out to do?

    Yes _____   No _____

4. Do you have any suggestions for improving this draft?

    _____

    _____

    _____

Step 2

Return each other's essays. Read your partner's evaluation. Discuss any questions you have with your partner.

Step 3

Now write a second draft, considering your partner's evaluation comments.

Evaluating the Second Draft

Step 1

Exchange your second drafts. Use the following questions to evaluate your partner's essay.

1. Look at how each of the body paragraphs is organized. Can you find the following parts?

Paragraph 1	topic sentence	yes	no
	bridge (optional)	yes	no
	support	yes	no
	conclusion	yes	no
Paragraph 2	topic sentence	yes	no
	bridge (optional)	yes	no
	support	yes	no
	conclusion	yes	no
Paragraph 3	topic sentence	yes	no
	bridge (optional)	yes	no
	support	yes	no
	conclusion	yes	no

2. Has the writer included an interpretation, and does the interpretation connect the ideas in the paragraph to the topic sentence?

    Paragraph 1   yes   no
    Paragraph 2   yes   no
    Paragraph 3   yes   no

3. Can the writer add anything more to further develop the body paragraphs? If so, explain.

    _____

    _____

    _____

    _____

    _____

4. Did the writer use words and expressions from Part 2, Language for Writing, in this essay? Give some examples:

    _____

    _____

    _____

5. Did the writer use them correctly?

    Yes _____   No _____

6. Do you have any suggestions for the writer in future work?

    _____

    _____

    _____

7. What did you particularly like about this essay?

    _____

    _____

    _____

Step 2

Return your second drafts. Read your partner's evaluation. Discuss any questions you have with your partner.

Writing the Final Draft

Now write a final draft, considering your partner's comments. Turn in this draft to your teacher.

Video Activities: College Graduation

Before You Watch.   Discuss these questions in small groups.

1. Have you ever attended a graduation ceremony? What happened at the ceremony?

2. How many years do people usually have to study to become doctors?

Watch.   Circle the correct answers to the following questions.

1. Why is Mrs. Christianson so happy?

    a. She's graduating from college.

    b. Her son is becoming a doctor.

    c. She has just immigrated to the United States.

2. Louis Christianson says that his mother gave him a love of _____.

    a. education   b. medicine   c. Mexico

3. Louis decided to become a doctor _____.

    a. when he was young

    b. in high school

    c. after high school

Watch Again.   Match the speakers to the quotations.

Quotations	Speakers
1. _____ I'd love to share with you some stories about the medical students soon to be physicians before you.	a. narrator
2. _____ I did a major in philosophy, so I had no plans to go to medical school.	b. graduation speaker
3. _____ Nine years ago Christianson was graduating from Madison High School.	c. Mr. Christianson
4. _____ I still see him as my baby.	d. Louis Christianson
5. _____ We are delighted.	e. Mrs. Christianson

After You Watch.   Write an essay about a graduation ceremony that you have attended. It can be your own graduation or someone else's. Give details about the feelings of the graduates and their families and friends.

Chapter 6

The Mind

IN THIS CHAPTER

You will learn about how dreams are interpreted and write about
an aspect of dreaming.

PART 1

Ideas for Writing

Getting Started

What do our dreams mean? Are they important messages to the dreamer? The art on these pages deals with sleep and dreaming.

1 Look at each picture, then answer the questions.

1. *The Nightmare*, Henry Fuseli

2. *The Dream of Reason Produces Monsters*, Francisco Goya

3. *With Dreams Upon My Bed*, William Blake

4. *The Dream of Fossian*, Ingres

1. Describe the four pictures. How does the title of each relate to what you see in the picture?

    _____

    _____

2. What do you think the dreamers of these pictures are dreaming about?

    _____

    _____

3. Describe how each picture makes you feel. Do any of them remind you of a dream you've had?

    _____

    _____

 **2** Interview a partner by asking the following questions.

1. When you dream, do you remember your dreams?
2. Are your dreams in color or in black and white?
3. Can you remember different dreams you've had at different points in your life?
4. Do you have any recurring dreams (dreams that happen over and over again)? What are they about?
5. Do you have any recurring themes or images in your dreams? What are they? (Some common recurring themes or images are water, animals, a house.)
6. Which of these common dream experiences have you had?
    a. being late for an important event
    b. losing a tooth
    c. flying
    d. falling
    e. being chased
    f. finding or losing valuables

3 Now combine your answers with those of your classmates in a survey. Can you draw any conclusions? For example:

■ Are women more likely to remember their dreams than men?

■ Are women more likely to dream in color?

■ Are there any differences (in general) between men's and women's dreams?

■ Do many students in your class dream in English?

■ Do you share any dream images or experiences with the other students?

Reading for Ideas

4 You are going to read a magazine article about recurring dreams and what they may mean. Answer the following questions before you read.

Prereading Questions

1. Have you ever tried to interpret a dream? Do you know of any rules or techniques for interpreting dreams?

    _____

    _____

2. Who was Sigmund Freud? What did he say about dreams?

    _____

    _____

Sigmund Freud

The Dream That Haunts You

For years, Helen Thacker has had the same distressing dream. "I'm trapped in a dark tunnel with men standing at the entrance waiting to attack me. When I scream for help, no sound comes out. I try again. A whisper. Finally, with all the strength I have, I yell." Suddenly, she's awake. "I can't tell you how terrifying that
5 dream is. Usually my heart pounds, and my body's wet with sweat. Sometimes I'm upset all through the next day."

Like Thacker, millions of people have recurring dreams that play inside their heads like scratched records. These dreams may be exhilarating—you fly down halls and over cities. Or they may be nightmares that jolt you into consciousness
10 after you've been chased, yet again, by giant bugs, vampires, or men with guns. Often the dreams have traumatic plots that leave you feeling upset in the morning. In one study of women's dreams by Rosalind Cartwright, Ph.D., a psychology and social sciences professor at Chicago's Rush-Presbyterian-St. Luke's

Medical Center, women describe nearly 50 percent of their recurring dreams as
15 "highly unpleasant" and only 8 percent as "strongly pleasant."

Ancient Greeks claimed dreams were messages from the gods. In the
Middle Ages, dreams supposedly marked visits from demons. Late nineteenth-
century doctors thought that nightmares came from difficulty breathing and a
reduced oxygen supply to the brain. Contemporary theorists have their own
20 explanations.

Some scientists believe all dreams are a physiological response to our
brain's nighttime activities. "They are simply our awareness of automatic acti-
vation of the brain during sleep," says J. Allen Hobson, M.D., a psychiatry professor at Harvard University and author of *The Dreaming Brain*. The brain stem
25 sends signals to the cortex (the center of vision and thought), and the cortex
turns those signals into dream stories. Your own experiences and emotions do
contribute to the dream, however. Stored in your memory, they organize the story
that you dream. "But dreaming is largely a random process," adds Dr. Hobson.
"A lot of the nonsense of dreams *is* nonsense."

30 Not so, say other experts who view repeated dreams as messages from a
person's deepest self, or the "royal road," as Freud wrote, to the unconscious.
"Dreams offer an unfailing view of the conflicts within a person," contends
Edward N. Brennan, M.D., an assistant professor of clinical psychiatry at Colum-
bia University. And they present that view through metaphors and symbols.

35 A woman who frequently dreams of being chased by men, for instance, may
unconsciously want closeness to a man but be afraid. Until she masters her
anxiety, her dreams will recur. Her response can be likened to a tongue probing
the roof of a mouth burned by hot food: "The dream keeps saying, 'This is where
it hurts,'" says Dr. Brennan. "And it will show you again and again and again."

40 Occasionally, recurring dreams may even predict the future, says Stanley
Krippner, Ph.D., a professor of psychology at San Francisco's Saybrook Institute
and coauthor of *Dream Telepathy*. He tells of one woman who kept dreaming
about a chandelier falling and crushing her baby in her crib. One night a clock
in the dream said 2 A.M. Frightened, the woman woke up and moved the baby
45 to her own bed. At 2 A.M. the chandelier crashed.

Of course, this mother may have unconsciously noted cracks in the ceiling
plaster or the danger of her infants' sleeping below a chandelier. "The brain puts
together a lot of little pieces of information and comes up with a [dream] conclusion that is sometimes very accurate," Dr. Krippner explains. But the dream
50 clock's 2 A.M. went beyond her five senses' perceptions. The image was either
precognition or just an educated guess.

"Dreams look out for our best interests," says Dr. Krippner. In some cases
they may even alert us to illness. In a study by Robert Smith, M.D., a professor
of psychiatry at Michigan State University in East Lansing, when cardiac pa-
55 tients reported death and separation dreams, often recurring, their hearts were
functioning poorly, but the patients did not know how sick they were.

Recurring dreams can also give advice. Consider the "be prepared" message tucked into the recurring dream of Linda Jo Bartholomew, a Stanford
University English lecturer: "I have a plane to catch, but instead of packing, I
60 clean the sink or polish shoes. The dream always makes me feel terrible that I've
planned so poorly," she admits.

What do recurring dreams mean? It depends on you and how each symbol
connects to your own life. Specific symbols have meanings unique to every

dreamer. A bow and arrow in a dream, for example, may stand for persecution,
65 but also for self-defense.

Because of the intimate relationship between you and what you dream,
"don't let anybody tell you what your dreams mean. Only you can know," says
Gayle Delaney, Ph.D., author of *Breakthrough Dreaming.* To decipher them, she
suggests writing a description of every image, then asking yourself: What real-
70 life situation resembles this dream?

Using that method, Iris McCarthy figured out a dream that recurred for five
years: "I was crouching in my kitchen. When the police came around a side gate
and saw me, they started shooting through the window. I could feel the bullets
sinking in my flesh." Who were the police? "My mother-in-law," says McCarthy,
75 a Mill Valley, California, housewife and mother of three. "Once, she did walk
around my house, looking through windows for me. I was always trying to es-
cape her wrath."

When interpreting repetitive dreams, watch for common symbols. Clothing
may indicate feelings about body image. Houses may represent your percep-
80 tion of your life. Cars, too, can reflect your life and whether you're going along
smooth or bumpy "roads."

Deborah Dembo, a pediatric nurse in Stanford, California, occasionally
dreams that her Honda is trapped in water or on a steep incline: "I can't drive
up higher or turn around and go back down. There's no way out." To her, the car
85 symbolizes freedom and independence, and so the dream could mean something in her life is "stuck."

—Kristin von Kreisler

Postreading Questions

5 Answer these questions.

1. What are some beliefs about dreaming that people held before the twentieth
   century?

2. What are two explanations for dreaming?

3. State in your own words at least three functions of recurring dreams,
   according to the article.

4. What is a possible explanation of the chandelier dream that supposedly predicted the future?

    _____

    _____

5. What do recurring dreams mean, according to the article?

    _____

    _____

6. How are we supposed to interpret recurring dream symbols, according to the article?

    _____

    _____

Thinking Critically

Interpreting Symbols

Postreading Questions 4 and 6 ask you to look for additional meanings or explanations beyond the literal meanings of certain events or symbols. This is called interpreting. Practice interpreting the dream symbols below. Then think of additional dream symbols and suggest interpretations for them.

Clothing   _____

House   _____

Cars   _____

_____   _____

_____   _____

_____   _____

Freewriting

6   Describe an interesting dream you've had and try to explain why you had it. If you don't remember a specific dream, think of a common "daydream" you have, or some thoughts you often have when awake.

Gathering Information

7 Find information on an aspect of dreaming that interests you. Look for information in books and magazines or do some searching online. Sample topics are:

- psychological dream interpretation (for example, Freud, Jung, humanistic psychology)
- nonpsychological or folk interpretation of dreams
- the importance of dreams in various cultures (for example, Native Americans, Senoi Malaysians, or your own culture)
- physiological aspects of dreaming

Take notes on your article and prepare to present your research results to the class.

8 In small groups, present the information you gathered from your reading about dreams. In your presentation, include:

- an explanation of how you obtained your information
- a visual that relates to your topic (this can be a photo, sketch, or picture)
- at least one question that helps your classmates relate to your topic

---

PART 2

Language for Writing

Interpreting Dreams

1 The following words and expressions from von Kreisler's article are useful when you discuss or write about interpreting dreams. Find these words and expressions in their original contexts in the article. Study how the expressions are used and take notes below on what each expressions means.

Verbs

1. to reflect something _____

2. to symbolize something or someone _____

3. to represent (mark, stand for, indicate) something _____

4. to dream of (about) something or someone _____

5. to have a dream about something or someone _____

6. to recur _____

7. to decipher _____

8. to interpret _____

Nouns

9. a dream image _____

10. a symbol _____

11. the unconscious _____

12. a metaphor _____

Adjectives

13. recurring _____

14. traumatic _____

Adverbs

15. unconsciously _____

2 Choose one of the works of art from page 98, and write a paragraph interpreting the dream images. Use the words and expressions presented in this section.

3 Consider again the dream you described in the Freewriting activity on page 103. Write a paragraph interpreting the dream again, this time using new words and expressions.

 **4** Choose two of the following dreams to interpret. Read them, think about them, and explain to a partner what you think they mean.

a. Boy, 5 years old: "I dreamed I was in the bathtub and the water began draining. My little sister went down the drain and just before she disappeared, she held her hand up. I caught it, and I pulled her out of the drain. I wasn't able to help our friend, Melanie, who went down the drain next. She didn't hold her hand up, so I couldn't save her."

b. Woman, 35 years old: "A common dream I had as a child was running away from an erupting volcano. The hot lava was creeping faster and faster toward me. I ran as fast as I could to avoid being trapped and burned by the lava. I always woke up from this dream out of breath and scared!"

c. Girl, 8 years old: "Last night I dreamed that a whole bunch of soldiers came into my bedroom through the window. There were carrying knives and guns and I was afraid they were going to kill me."

d. Man, 50 years old: "I often dream that I've enrolled in a class and forget when it starts and where it's located. In the dream I'm wandering around campus looking for the correct building and feeling quite lost. I feel very guilty in this dream."

PART 3

Systems for Writing

Paragraph Organization: Levels of Generality

Review Point

■ In a well-developed paragraph, the writer organizes ideas in logical order and explains how the supporting information is connected to the main idea.

New Points

An effective way to organize ideas in a paragraph is to use specific facts and illustrations to support general statements. Here are two ways to organize your ideas:

■ **Top-down** organization
■ **Divided** organization

Choose the pattern that best fits what you are writing about.

Look at the following example of **top-down** organization. It looks like a set of stairs and each idea in the paragraph moves one step down in generality.

1				Topic sentence (most general idea)
2				More specific information about the topic
	3			More specific information about Sentence 2
		4		More specific information about Sentence 3
			5	More specific information about Sentence 4

The following example, **divided** organization, looks like two sets of stairs, as the topic sentence of the paragraph has two parts.

1			Topic sentence (most general; may have two or more parts)
2			First part (more specific)
	3		Fact or illustration related to the first part (very specific)
		4	More specific information about Sentence 3
2			Second part (same level of specificity as the first part)
	3		Fact or illustration related to the second part (very specific)
		4	More specific information about Sentence 3

Organizing your ideas often begins at the brainstorming stage when you have a list of ideas on a topic. Before you are ready to write, you must recognize the general-to-specific relationships of the ideas in your notes. Look at the following list of ideas related to the topic of anthropology as an academic field. Then notice the general-to-specific organization of the ideas indicated by the numbers in the second list.

Notes

Anthropology   The Study of Primates

            Cultural Anthropology

The Great Apes   The Study of Linguistics

            Physical Anthropology

                        Native American Languages

General-to-Specific Organization

1 Anthropology

    2 Physical Anthropology

        3 The study of primates

            4 The great apes

    2 Cultural Anthropology

        3 The study of linguistics

            4 Native American languages

Note that "anthropology" is the most general idea; it is like the topic sentence of a paragraph. "Physical anthropology" and "cultural anthropology" are next in degree of generality, as they are the two major subdivisions of the general idea. "The study of primates" and "the study of linguistics" are labeled level 3, as each gives more specific information about the level 2 ideas. "The great apes" and "Native American languages" are very specific ideas about the level 3 ideas.

1   Try this general-to-specific organization of ideas yourself. The following is a list of ideas on the study of dreams in no special order. Study it, then organize the ideas in a general-to-specific pattern.

Notes

Dream interpretation: literal or symbolic

Example—dream of one's mother or friend

Dream of someone or something not found in one's day-to-day life—symbolic

Dream of someone or something in real life—literal

Example—dream of a dragon or some other fantastic animal

General-to-Specific Organization

1 _____

  2 _____

    3 _____

  2 _____

    3 _____

2   Now, study this general-to-specific organization of ideas in the context of an entire paragraph. Read the following paragraph and answer the questions that follow.

(1) According to one author, dreams can have either a literal or a symbolic interpretation. (2) If a dream image represents someone the dreamer knows or an event that has actually occurred in the dreamer's life, then this image can be taken literally. (3) For example, if a person dreams of his or her mother, then most likely the dream is indeed about the person's mother, and the mother image should not be taken to represent anyone or anything else. (4) However, if a dream image does not represent a person or a thing that can be found in the dreamer's day-to-day existence, then the image can be taken as a symbol of something else. (5) For example, if a person dreams of a dragon or some other exotic animal he or she never comes in contact with, then the dreamer is free to interpret this image as a symbol of something else. (6) Therefore, when interpreting dreams, this author recommends looking for symbols only when a literal interpretation is impossible.

1. What is the topic of the first sentence?

    _____

    Is this idea general or specific?

    _____

2. What idea is expressed in Sentence 2?

    _____

    How does the idea in Sentence 2 relate to the idea of the first sentence?

    _____

3. What is the relationship, if any, of Sentence 4 to Sentence 2?

    _____

4. What is the relationship of Sentence 4 to the first sentence?

    _____

5. Explain the relationships of Sentences 3 and 5 to the rest of the paragraph.

    _____

6. What is the function of Sentence 6?

    _____

If you were to diagram the ideas of this paragraph as you did the preceding ideas on anthropology, the pattern would look like this:

1		Interpreting dreams (literal or symbolic meaning)
	2	Definition of literal interpretation
		3 Example of literal interpretation
	2	Definition of symbolic interpretation
		3 Example of symbolic interpretation
1		Conclusion

Note how all the ideas in this paragraph relate logically to each other in a general-to-specific pattern.

Focus on Testing

"Drawing" Your Ideas

In several places in this chapter, you read about organizational patterns that can be represented visually. Using lines, drawing a sketch, or making a diagram or chart is often a fast way to plan the relationships between main points in your essay. This will help you save time when writing under pressure.

3 Read the paragraph and study the relationships between ideas in the sentences. Number each sentence according to its level of generality. The most general ideas will be numbered 1, and the most specific ideas will be 3.

( ) In the last several decades, researchers have learned a great deal about the frequency and duration of dreams, which can be observed in two ways. ( ) One way is to connect wires from an amplifying and recording device, called an electroencephalograph, to the sleeper's head. ( ) This instrument registers "brain waves," which are tiny changes in the electrical potential of the brain at rest. ( ) A certain pattern of these brain waves indicates dreaming. ( ) Another way scientists collect data on dreams is by observing the sleeper's eyes. ( ) There is active eye movement when a person dreams. ( ) This eye movement can be seen through closed eyelids and recorded automatically on moving paper tape. ( ) From these two methods, scientists have found that everyone dreams four to six times a night and that each dream lasts between fifteen and twenty minutes. ( ) If you don't think you dream, you simply don't remember your dreams!

4 Study the notes and organizational pattern on the topic of anthropology on page 107. Write a well-organized, well-developed paragraph from them. You should have at least eight sentences in your paragraph, but you may have more. You may add new ideas if you like. If you need more information on the topic, brainstorm with a partner.

5   Write two paragraphs on a folk belief or saying about dreams from your country or another country. For the first paragraph, use the top-down organizational pattern:

            1
              2
                3
                  4
                    5
                       6 (optional)
        Conclusion

Note that you will be giving increasingly specific information about your main idea as you proceed. Your paragraph will have five or six sentences. Make sure that you include all the levels of generality shown in the preceding diagram. Then rewrite the paragraph using this divided organizational pattern:

            1
              2
                3
                  4
              2
                3
                  4
        Conclusion

Note that in this paragraph you will be giving increasingly specific information about two aspects of your main idea. This paragraph will be at least eight sentences long. Make sure that you include all the levels of generality shown in the outline above.

   When you have finished, exchange paragraphs with a partner and answer the following questions.

1.   What is the difference between the two paragraphs in terms of organization and development of ideas? Are there any other differences between the two?

     _____

     _____

2.   Which paragraph do you like better? Why?

     _____

     _____

3.   Is the topic of these paragraphs better suited to a top-down or divided pattern of organization? Explain your answer.

     _____

     _____

6   Choose a paragraph from the body of one of your previous essays. Reread it and see how well it is organized. Try to diagram it as you did the preceding paragraph. If you cannot diagram it, rewrite it, paying attention to its organizational pattern.

Writing Assignments

Write an essay on one of the following topics. Use the ideas you've discussed and the material you've written so far in this chapter as the basis of your essay.

1. Are dreams important? Why or why not?

2. Describe a folk belief about dreams from your culture or another culture.

3. Write your reaction to the following quotation:

    Dreams show wisdom that the dreamer does not even know he has!
    —Paraphrased from *Paracelsus*

4. Write an essay on any aspect of dreaming that interests you.

PART 4

Evaluating for Rewriting

Evaluating the First Draft

Step 1

Choose a partner and exchange your essays. Read your partner's first draft to get the general idea; don't focus on specific details or on grammar or punctuation. Use the following questions to evaluate each other's essays.

1. What is the main idea?

    _____

    _____

2. What is the writer's purpose in writing this essay?

    _____

    _____

3. Did the writer accomplish what she or he set out to do?

    Yes _____   No _____

4. Do you have any suggestions for improving this first draft?

    _____

    _____

Step 2

Return each other's essays. Read your partner's evaluation. Discuss any questions you have with your partner.

Step 3

Now write a second draft, considering your partner's evaluation comments.

Evaluating the Second Draft

Step 1

Exchange your second drafts. Use the following questions to evaluate your partner's essay.

1. Find the first body paragraph of the essay. Read the topic sentence of this paragraph. What is the main idea?

   _____

   _____

2. Could one of the two organizational patterns discussed in this chapter be used for a paragraph with this main idea? If so, which one (top-down or divided)?

   _____

   _____

3. Now read the rest of the paragraph. Was your answer to Question 2 correct?

   Yes _____   No _____

4. Using a pencil, number each sentence in the paragraph to show how each relates to the preceding one. Was this easy or difficult to do? Why?

   _____

   _____

5. How many level 3 sentences (examples and facts) does the paragraph have?

   _____

   _____

   Briefly list the ideas in the level 3 sentences used in this paragraph:

   _____

   _____

Were any level 2 sentences not followed by level 3 sentences?

Yes _____   No _____

If so, make suggestions for improvement.

6. Were there any level 4 or 5 sentences in this paragraph? If so, what was their function?

_____

_____

Now answer these same six questions about the remaining body paragraphs in the essay.

7. How many words and expressions from Part 2, Language for Writing, did the writer use in this essay?

_____

8. Were they used correctly in terms of both meaning and grammar?

Yes _____   No _____

9. What are the strengths of this essay?

_____

_____

Step 2

Return your second drafts. Read your partner's evaluation. Discuss any questions you have with your partner.

Writing the Final Draft

Now write a final draft, considering your partner's comments. Turn in this draft to your teacher.

Video Activities: Social Phobia

Before You Watch. Answer these questions in small groups.

1. A phobia is _____.

    a. a need   b. a fear   c. an idea

2. What kinds of phobias do you know of?

Watch. Answer these questions in small groups.

1. What kind of phobia does Katherine Whizmore suffer from?

    _____

2. Circle the things that people with this disorder believe.

    a. People are judging them all of the time.

    b. People want to physically hurt them.

    c. People are unfair to them.

3. Which kinds of treatments help these people?

    a. education about their illness

    b. antidepressant drugs and behavioral therapy

    c. surgery

Watch Again. Choose the correct answers.

1. By the age of 20, Katherine Whizmore was afraid to _____.

    a. go to work   b. cross the street   c. go shopping alone

2. How many Americans suffer from this disease?

    a. 100 million   b. 1 million   c. 10 million

3. This disease usually begins in _____.

    a. college   b. high school   c. junior high school

4. _Panicked_ means _____.

    a. confident   b. very frightened   c. sick

5. _Impaired_ means _____.

    a. afraid   b. extraordinary   c. injured

6. _Scrutiny_ means _____.

    a. correction   b. inspection   c. destruction

7. *Harshly* means _____.

   a. fairly　　　　　　b. kindly　　　　　　c. cruelly

8. *Struggle* means to _____.

   a. fight　　　　　　b. give up　　　　　　c. win

After You Watch.   Write an essay about a time when you felt afraid, shy, or embarrassed. What happened to make you feel that way? What did you do about it?

Chapter 7

Working

IN THIS CHAPTER

You will interview a businessperson and write about an aspect of working in today's world.

<table>
<tr><td>PART 1</td></tr>
</table>

Ideas for Writing

Getting Started

1 Think about what it might be like to work with people from different cultures. Then study the pictures below and answer the questions that follow.

1.

2.

3.

4.

5.

1. What are people probably doing in each of the photos?

_____

_____

_____

_____

_____

_____

2. What communication problems do you think might occur in these situations?

_____

_____

_____

_____

_____

_____

 2 Read each sentence. Circle A if you agree with it and D if you disagree with it. Compare your answers with those of your classmates.

1. A   D   When a company hires a new employee, they should take into consideration the person's personal relationships with others in the company; this is more important than job qualifications.

2. A   D   Time equals money: it's important to get things done quickly.

3. A   D   Teamwork is very important.

4. A   D   Employees should discuss their problems with their supervisors frequently.

5. A   D   Personal relationships are very important in any business transaction.

6. A   D   Written contracts and agreements are not necessary; a person's word is enough in making a business deal.

7. A   D   Individual employees are responsible for the success of their company as a whole, not just for their own work.

8. A   D   Employees should always show respect when they talk to people in higher positions.

9. A   D   A person's sex or race should not influence whether or not a company should hire him or her.

10. A   D   Only the manager should make decisions that affect his or her employees, not the employees themselves.

Reading for Ideas

3   The following reading selection is an excerpt from a book by Alison Lanier titled *The Rising Sun on Main Street: Working with the Japanese*. In this excerpt, Lanier discusses an aspect of Japanese management style, decision making by consensus (group decision making). She compares the Japanese style to the American style. Before you read, answer the questions in small groups.

Prereading Questions

1. What do you know about Japanese business culture? What do you know about American business culture?

    _____

    _____

    _____

    _____

    _____

2. How do businesspeople usually make decisions in another culture you are familiar with? As a group? Or does one person make the decision? Does decision making take a long time? Why or why not?

    _____

    _____

    _____

    _____

    _____

Decision by Consensus

One of the most important differences in management style between the Japanese and most other countries lies in the area of decision-making. Westerners often find the Japanese method of making decisions to be extremely slow. However, most people do not realize the different thought processes and
5 procedures that are going on during Japanese-style decision making.

Westerners tend to make major decisions at the top, in board meetings, among department heads (high-level managers). They then "pass the word" down to lower-level managers and others, to implement and carry out the decision. The Japanese do the opposite. Their system, commonly known as *ringi,*
10 is the corporate version of "government by consensus."

With *ringi*, decisions are not made "on high" and given to lower-level employees to be implemented. Rather, they are proposed from below and move upward. In this process, the decision receives additional input and approvals after much discussion through all levels of the company.

15 "One should think of the system as a filter through which ideas pass," says Robert T. Moran. "The whole process, as it slowly goes through various levels of the company, can last from two to three weeks to a matter of months. Each level takes its own time to consider the details. If the matter is complex or sensitive, it can take even longer."

20 For decisions that are not of really major importance, approvals can be given by various individuals (or by groups). But when any decision is of great importance, the Japanese look for broad consensus. *Ringi* should be seen as a "process" rather than a system. It gives management the choice of a broad selection of practical choices. Often, the person who initiates an idea is a sec-
25 tion chief. He proposes an idea (which may have been suggested to him by one of his workers). He gets his section members to research it; they all discuss it. When satisfied, he passes it up to the higher levels of management.

Even junior members take part in all this deliberation. It is considered part of their training. It is also a way to develop company motivation. The idea is
30 considered all the way up until it reaches the president. If he approves it, it will have been seen and considered by almost everyone who could be in any way involved in the final implementation. One can imagine the bargaining, persuasion, trading of favors, seeking of support, and general "lobbying" that goes on throughout the process! All of this is known as *nemawashi,* which means "bind-
35 ing up the roots." (This suggests the image of a tree that will survive only if everything is properly prepared in advance.)

One of the major benefits of *ringi* is that it avoids the possibility of any one person being "personally responsible" for a decision. When responsibility is spread out to many people, no one "loses face" (is embarrassed).

40 "Sometimes the delays in making even simple decisions are almost unbearable," said a fast-moving American executive who works with a worldwide hotel chain. "Everybody has to be involved with everything," he continued. "It takes forever. As far as I am concerned, this is without a doubt the very hardest part of working for a Japanese company. You feel as if you can never get a decision
45 on anything, large or small."

"By the time the decision is finally made," added another, "I have usually lost interest in it and am involved in something else."

If you try to hurry the process, it does more harm than good. The Japanese do not like pressure. Obviously, frustrated Westerners will be itching to know
50 what is going on as the silence continues for weeks or months. You submit a proposal or an inquiry. Nothing happens. Who is holding it up? What is happening? Did the message ever get through?

If the decision that you are waiting for relates to a new idea, perhaps something you have initiated, then you can count on a really long delay. If, on the other
55 hand, the company is merely talking about changes to an idea that they have already agreed to, then it may take considerably less time for a reply.

But you will rarely get quick action unless, as one experienced businessperson said, "You have gold that is $7.00 on the open market and are willing to sell it for $6.00. Then you will get action without delay." You may oc-
60 casionally meet Japanese who will try to shorten the normal time in consideration of Western impatience. But don't expect it.

In writing this book, I asked several businesspeople who work well with the Japanese what they think is the single biggest factor in their success. In every single case the first quality that they mentioned was "patience, patience, and
65 still more patience." They all agreed: "If you lose your patience or get upset, you are likely to leave without accomplishing anything."

Although the *ringi* system is slow, no one can complain afterwards. The result is harmonious feelings and bad feelings are lessened—if not eliminated, because when the process has reached a certain stage, no one feels he can
70 "buck the tide." So, he goes along with it. After that, he is effectively silenced. Direct opposition is rarely effective among the Japanese. One achieves more by the persuading and negotiating—one might say "lobbying"—that is allowed through *nemawashi.*

Actually, the delay that happens before a decision is made may not be as
75 great as it sometimes appears when compared with Western systems. Where the Western "top-down" approach to decision making is used, the original plan or agreement is frequently made relatively quickly at the top in the boardroom. However, delays of weeks or months may follow while lower-level employees first learn about the decision and are then persuaded to support it. Both steps
80 are necessary before a plan can actually be implemented. When lower-level employees have not participated in making the decision, misunderstandings, disagreement, or other delays frequently occur.

In Japan, in contrast, once the decision is finally made, all relevant staff members understand it thoroughly. They are familiar with it because they were
85 involved with it in the early stages. So, although it may take a long time to arrive at the decision, once approval has been given, they can implement it rapidly and smoothly. The final time difference between the two systems, therefore, may not be as far apart as it can sometimes seem.

Furthermore, in the Japanese system, people in lower-level positions feel
90 they have been involved. They have been able—often urged—to suggest proposals, projects, or refinements. Japanese bosses believe in encouraging suggestions from the lower-level employees. The idea of creating a consensus that incorporates everyone on the organization is at the heart of Japanese business philosophy and methods.

Postreading Questions

4   Answer these questions.

1. Based on your and your classmates' knowledge of Japanese business culture and Western business culture, do you think that Lanier has presented a correct picture of the Japanese decision-making process?

    _____

    _____

2. Explain in your own words the basic differences between the American decision-making process and that of the Japanese.

    _____

    _____

    _____

3. In paragraphs 8 and 9, Lanier quotes American businesspeople's opinions of *ringi*. However, she doesn't quote any Japanese businesspeople's opinions of the American system. Pretend that you are a Japanese businessperson. You are doing business in the United States with an American company. The company is going through a decision-making process. The decision affects you. What would you say about the American decision-making process?

    _____

    _____

    _____

    _____

4. Compare the Japanese decision-making process to that of another culture. Is it different? If so, how is it different? Give examples.

    _____

    _____

    _____

5. Practice making a decision by consensus. In groups of five or six, make a decision with the entire group about one of the following topics. Create a consensus, making sure everyone in the group is involved. Then, if possible, implement your decision. Afterward, discuss how you felt about the consensus process.

    - Decide on a new seating arrangement in your class.
    - Decide on a Freewriting topic for this chapter.
    - Decide if and/or when to take a break during class.
    - Decide if and when to have a class party.
    - Your topic: _____

Thinking Critically

Making Inferences

The author of "Decision by Consensus" discusses the advantages and disadvantages of the Japanese decision-making process. She has an American point of view. Although she doesn't directly discuss the advantages and disadvantages of the *American* decision-making process, based on other material in the excerpt, you can infer (guess) what they are.

Practice making inferences by summarizing the two systems in the following chart. You will have to infer the American advantages and disadvantages based on the material in the excerpt.

	Ringi	**American Decision-Making Process**
Advantages		
Disadvantages		

Freewriting

5 If you decided on a Freewriting topic in item 5 on page 123, write about that topic for twenty minutes without stopping. If you didn't, write for twenty minutes without stopping on the difficulties that you might have doing business in a foreign country. You can write about doing business in the United States, Japan, or any country whose culture or business practices you are familiar with.

Gathering Information

6 Conduct an interview in which you ask a businessperson to describe the practices and policies that he or she thinks are important for a company to be successful. Include questions such as the following, and some of your own:

■ What employee benefits are there? (for example, health insurance, stock in the company, other employee benefits and/or services such as transportation to and from work, and so on).

■ What management styles are used? How do managers inspire employees? Do lower-level employees participate in decision making?

■ What are the hiring and firing policies?

■ What's it like to work there? Are the offices nice? Is the equipment modern?

■ How are the relationships among employees?

7 Share the results of your interview with the class. Organize your presentation around the answer to the following question: What policies and practices ensure success in a business?

PART 2   # Language for Writing

Describing Work in a Multicultural Setting

1   The author of "Decision by Consensus" uses many words and expressions that are useful in writing about business styles. Use the following definitions and line numbers to find them in context in the article. Then write the word or expression on the lines next to its meaning.

1. a way of getting work done and/or getting others to get work done, especially in a large corporation (Line 1) = _____

2. tell others (Line 7) = _____

3. to accomplish (Line 8) = _____

4. at the higher levels (Line 11) = _____

5. political (Line 19) = _____

6. discussion (Line 28) = _____

7. persuading (Line 33) = _____

8. started (Line 54) = _____

9. the condition of being in agreement (Line 68) = _____

10. made smaller or less important (Line 68) = _____

11. improvements (Line 91) = _____

Describing Causes and Effects

2   At least one of the assignments for this chapter asks you to discuss causes or effects or both. Study the following expressions and notice which expressions introduce causes and which introduce effects (A = cause, B = effect).

Expressions	Examples
B *results from* A.	Harmony <u>results from</u> the practice of ringi.
A *results in* B.	The ringi system <u>results in</u> harmony.
A *causes* B.	The ringi system <u>causes</u> harmony.
B *is the result of* A.	Harmony <u>is the result of</u> the ringi system.
Because of A, B.	<u>Because of</u> ringi, power struggles are minimized.

3   Write a paragraph based on your topic for the Freewriting assignment on page 124. Use words and expressions from this section.

4   Write one or more paragraphs about the interview you conducted in the Gathering Information section on page 124. Use words and expressions from this section.

5   Write a paragraph about the causes or effects of a cultural misunderstanding in a business or educational situation. Use words and expressions from this section.

PART 3	# Systems for Writing

Cause and Effect

Review Point

■ The organizational pattern you choose for an essay depends on the topic of the essay.

New Points

■ An effective way of making a point in an essay is to show causal relationships.

■ You can describe a causal relationship in a sentence, a paragraph, or an entire essay.

■ There are two kinds of causal relationships: a simple one where one action leads to another (a → b), and a complex one where one cause leads to one result, which leads to another result (a → b → c). This is called a *causal chain*.

Look at these examples of the two types of causal relationships:

Sentence 1:
$$a$$
The rise in global business has increased →
$$b$$
the need to understand cultural interactions within organizations.

Sentence 2:
$$a$$
A lack of knowledge about cross-cultural negotiations
$$b$$
can lead to → misunderstanding in a business transaction
$$c$$
that can result in → loss of profits in the long run.

---

1 Sentences 1 and 2 describe causes and effects. Which words or expressions indicate causes and which words or expressions indicate effects? Make a list of these.

Causes	Effects
_____	_____
_____	_____
_____	_____

2 A causal chain can be as long as necessary to cover all the important causes and effects of your subject. Complete the following chains by adding the missing information. Use your imagination.

1. don't pay attention in class → can't complete homework → _____ → _____

2. _____ → willing to take risks → _____ → _____

3. _____ → _____ → getting a job in an American company → _____

4. _____ → _____ → _____ → learn to speak a foreign language fluently

Causal Chain Essay Organization I

New Points

- The thesis statement of a causal chain essay presents the initial cause and final result; the body paragraphs explain the process from cause to result in detail.

- There are many ways to organize a causal chain; however, in order for the chain to be the subject of an entire essay, there must be enough intermediate steps to make up at least two body paragraphs.

Look at this diagram of one possible organizational pattern for developing an essay showing a causal chain:

    I.   Introduction

         Thesis Statement: a → f

    II.   a → b → c

   III.   d → e → f

   IV.   Conclusion

Now, read the following thesis statement for an essay. Then read the six steps in the causal chain that the writer will develop.

---

a → b → c → d → e → f

A lack of awareness of the differences between men's and women's speech can lead to discrimination in the work place.

                      a

A lack of awareness of men's and women's speech differences

        b   c

→ misinterpretation → lack of confidence

           d   e

→ decreased responsibilities → no opportunities to exhibit skills

             f

→ no promotion (which is discriminatory)

Causal Chain Essay Organization II

New Point

■ Another way to organize a causal chain essay is to begin with the final result and work backward to the initial cause.

3 Read the following example of a thesis statement for this type of essay organization:

> John ended up resigning from his position in the company and returning to the United States as a result of his lack of knowledge about Japanese business styles.

Based on what you've learned about Japanese and American business styles in this chapter, write causes that could be included as intermediate steps in the development of this essay.

John's lack of knowledge about Japanese business styles

_____ →

_____ →

_____ →

_____ →

_____ →

John resigned from his job.

Focus on Testing

Having a Repertoire of Organizational Patterns

Part 3 presents two ways of organizing a cause-and-effect essay. Knowing two or three organizational patterns for a particular essay type will help you plan and write essays faster in test-taking situations.

4 Practice developing a causal chain in the following oral exercise with your class-mates. Begin with the single cause provided below and take it as far as possible by having individual students give direct and logical results that then lead to further results. How long can you make your causal chain?

Initial cause: Traveling to another country   →   _____

→ _____   →   _____   →   _____

→ _____   →   _____   →   and so on.

5 Write a thesis statement for a causal-chain essay based on the reading on pages 121–122.

_____

_____

_____

_____

_____

6 Read the following sentences. They describe situations that are either causes or effects. Then develop a causal chain based on each situation. From each causal chain, develop a thesis statement and an organizational outline for an essay. Share your answers with a partner and discuss any differences you find.

Ben attends Spanish class every day.   (cause)

Rica understands English grammar but cannot speak English.   (effect)

David Livingstone felt very comfortable traveling alone in the African wilderness.   (cause)

7 Rewrite Activity 3 from Part 2, page 125, using what you've learned in this part.

Writing Assignments

Write an essay on one of the following topics. Use the ideas you've discussed and written about so far in this chapter and previous chapters as the basis for your essay. Although each of the assignments can be organized according to the pattern of a causal chain, you may choose to organize your essay differently. If you write more than one essay, practice causal-chain organization at least once.

1. To what extent should a large corporation be concerned with the welfare of its employees, the environment, or society as a whole? You can discuss all of these or choose only one.

2. What practices and policies contribute to success in a multicultural organization? You may write about the practices and policies that contribute to success in a multicultural college, school, or classroom, if you wish.

3. What policies and practices in a large corporation lead to employee satisfaction?

4. Explain, agree with, or disagree with the following quotation:

"People are motivated by three things in terms of doing work. One is money, another is a desire to be helpful, and the third is a need to be creative."

—*Michele Williams*, from *Working Free*, by John Applegath

5. Compare two businesses or organizations that you are familiar with. Consider the companies' concern for their employees, the environment, and society, as well as their degree of financial success.

6. Write about any aspect of working in a multicultural environment that interests you.

PART 4 # Evaluating for Rewriting

Evaluating the First Draft

Step 1

Choose a partner and exchange your essays. Read your partner's first draft to get the general idea; don't focus on specific details or on grammar or punctuation. Use the questions here and on the next page to evaluate each other's essays.

1. What is the main idea?

_____

_____

_____

2. What is the writer's purpose in writing this essay?

_____

_____

_____

3. Did the writer accomplish what he or she set out to do?

Yes _____   No _____

4. Do you have any suggestions for improving this first draft?

_____

_____

_____

Step 2

Return each other's essays. Read your partner's evaluation. Discuss any questions you have with your partner.

Step 3

Now write a second draft, considering your partner's evaluation comments.

Evaluating the Second Draft

Step 1

Exchange your second drafts. Use the following questions to evaluate your partner's essay.

1. Write the thesis statement below and, on the basis of the thesis, predict what the writer will discuss.

   Thesis: _____

   _____

   Prediction: _____

   _____

   _____

2. On the basis of the thesis statement, predict how the essay will be organized. Write the organizational pattern here:

   _____

   _____

   _____

   _____

   _____

   _____

   _____

   _____

   Now read the rest of the essay.

3. If the essay is organized in the pattern of a causal chain, write the causal chain below.

_____ → _____ → _____ → _____
and so on.

4. Does the writer adequately demonstrate the causal relationship among all the elements of the chain?

Yes _____   No _____

If not, give suggestions for improvement.

_____

_____

_____

5. Did the writer use words and expressions from Part 2, Language for Writing, in this essay? Give some examples:

_____

_____

_____

6. Did the writer use them correctly?

Yes _____   No _____

7. Do you have any suggestions for the writer in future work?

_____

_____

_____

8. What did you particularly like about this essay?

_____

_____

_____

Step 2

Return your second drafts. Read your partner's evaluation. Discuss any questions you have with your partner.

Writing the Final Draft

Now write a final draft, considering your partner's comments. Turn in this draft to your teacher.

Video Activities: Telecommuting

Before You Watch.   Sometimes people work from home. What are some advantages and disadvantages of telecommuting? List them below. In small groups, discuss your answers.

Advantages to Workers	Advantages to Employers
1. _____	1. _____
2. _____	2. _____
3. _____	3. _____

Disadvantages to Workers	Disadvantages to Employers
1. _____	1. _____
2. _____	2. _____
3. _____	3. _____

Watch.   Take notes on the benefits of telecommuting from different perspectives.

1. As you listen, note the benefits of telecommuting from a worker's perspective.

    _____

    _____

2. As you listen, note the benefits of telecommuting from an employer's perspective.

    _____

    _____

Watch Again.   Answer these questions in small groups.

1. Listen for these numbers and write what each one represents.
    a. 20,000,000 _____   c. 10,000 _____
    b. 12,000–13,000 _____   d. 3,000–4,000 _____

2. The phrases *gridlock* and *bumper-to-bumper* refer to _____.
    a. traffic accidents   b. slow traffic   c. very heavy traffic

3. When someone is *goofing off,* they are _____.
    a. sleeping   b. working   c. playing

4. The expression *saving a bundle* means _____.
    a. saving a lot of money
    b. working harder
    c. getting work done faster

5. Another word for *telecommuter* is _____.
    a. telephoner   b. telenetter   c. teleworker

After You Watch.   Write an essay explaining why you would or would not want to telecommute. What would be the advantages? What would be the disadvantages?

Chapter 8

Breakthroughs

IN THIS CHAPTER

You will gather information on breakthroughs in solar energy and write about a source of energy that interests you.

Ideas for Writing

Getting Started

Solar power production and applications are becoming more accessible and less expensive.

1   Look at these photos that show current applications of solar power. Then answer the questions in small groups.

1. Solar panels heat water and provide electricity.

2. Folding solar panel provides power for his laptop computer.

3. Solar energy can provide power for cars.

4. Solar-powered watches are becoming more common.

6. Solar-powered toys are fun and energy-efficient.

5. Solar radios are portable and convenient.

7. Solar-powered bicycles are part bike, part scooter.

8. Solar-powered lamps can save cities money.

1. Which of the examples of solar power pictured in these photos have you seen before?

_____

_____

2. What additional applications of solar power have you seen or used?

_____

_____

3. What are some of the conditions that must exist for solar power to work?

_____

_____

4. How does solar power work? Try to give a brief explanation to your group members.

_____

_____

2   In small groups, discuss the advantages and disadvantages of each energy source listed below. Which ones are expensive? Efficient? Difficult to build? Require special weather conditions? Require special equipment? What are the potential hazards of each energy source? Record your answers in the following chart.

Energy Source	Advantages	Disadvantages
1. wind		
2. sun		
3. oil		
4. coal		
5. nuclear fission		
6. hydroelectric power		
7. geothermal power		

Reading for Ideas

3   You are going to read an article about a breakthrough in solar power in Australia. Before you read, answer these questions.

Prereading Questions

1. What do you know about the conditions for solar power in Australia? Would solar power be possible or important there? Why?

    _____

    _____

2. What is a photovoltaic cell? a photovoltaic panel?

    _____

    _____

3. What do you think a modular inverter is? First, use your knowledge of word parts to guess the meaning, then consult a dictionary.

    _____

    _____

4. Complete this sentence by supplying the missing words:

    Solar energy uses _____ to create _____ .

5. What is rooftop solar electricity?

    _____

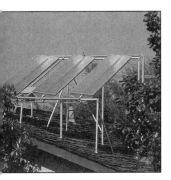

Solar Electricity Innovation

After more than two years of development, rooftop solar electricity became a real option when an innovative modular inverter passed its final compliance test in Australia.

The new modular inverter is a unique and innovative rooftop product that
5 generates clean green electricity without any moving parts, noise, or pollution. It does this using the photovoltaic (PV) effect. Just 1 kilowatt (kW) on an average rooftop in Australia takes up less than 10 square meters and saves up to 50 tons of carbon dioxide emissions over its 25-year life.

The project's managing director said, "At the beginning, we didn't realize
10 how expensive it would be to develop affordable rooftop Solar Photovoltaics (PV). We had to meet requirements for product safety, power quality, radio interference, wiring rules, building codes and electricity grid-connection." All the technical barriers to mass production have now been overcome and Australia is a step closer to being a significant participant in the global solar industry, the
15 fastest growing energy industry today with a growth rate last year of 30%.

In response to the increased danger of global warming, there is potential for the Australian solar PV industry to create 3,000 jobs by 2010 and annual revenues of $705 million. The modular inverter technology will help shift interest away from conventional utilities and help homeowners who have environmental
20 concerns.

Meanwhile, Australian researchers continue to pursue the development of its thin-film, PV solar cell technology which promises to significantly reduce the cost of solar PV panels. In regard to this world leading effort, Professor Martin Green said, "In only five years we have accomplished what has taken interna-
25 tional teams working on alternative approaches more than 20 years. With about one hundredth the funding and a quarter of the time, our cells are now higher in performance than the best commercial modules of the most developed thin-film alternative. It is significant that this performance has been achieved by depositing only a tenth of the thin-film material originally anticipated onto glass.
30 This gives the technology a significant cost advantage."

Postreading Questions

4   Answer these questions.

1. What is the solar power breakthrough in Australia? Why is it innovative?

   _____

   _____

2. What is the biggest obstacle to developing solar energy for widespread use?

   _____

   _____

3. What two facts did you learn about the Australian solar power industry?

   _____

   _____

4. The article refers to another project solar power technologists are working to develop. What is this?

   _____

   _____

Thinking Critically

Expanding the Literal Meanings of Words

In the article you just read, some words are used in new ways. You may not be able to find these definitions in the dictionary. Always use context to help you understand how familiar words take on new meanings. Practice doing this by reviewing some of the phrases from the reading selection. Write your own explanations of what these mean.

1. became a real option

   _____

2. passed its final compliance test

   _____

3. generates clean green electricity

   _____

4. Australia is a step closer to being a significant participant in the global solar industry

   _____

5. homeowners who have environmental concerns

   _____

Freewriting

5   Write for twenty minutes on your response to the article and your opinion of solar energy.

Gathering Information

6   In small groups, collect information on breakthroughs with solar energy. Organize your information on a poster that you can display in class. Collect photos, drawings, and diagrams as you do your research. Include information in each of these categories:

   ■ Description of the breakthrough/how you got the information
   ■ What it looks like/how it works
   ■ Cost of production/cost of use
   ■ How it compares to previous versions
   ■ Public reaction
   ■ Your opinion and predictions

7 Alternative energy is a controversial topic. Is it the answer to our energy problems, or will it create even greater problems in the future? Is it worth the expense? As a class, hold a debate in which you argue the advantages of one or more sources of energy. First, develop a statement, or resolution, which expresses the opinion to be argued. Then divide into teams and develop the arguments for your side. You can use the information you gathered in the previous activity. Develop at least three major arguments for your side and prepare at least three arguments to counter what you predict the other side will say. A debate is usually structured as follows:

First Team	**Second Team**
1. Presents opening statement	2. Presents opening statement
3. Presents three major arguments	4. Presents three major arguments
5. Presents three counterarguments	6. Presents three counter arguments
7. Makes closing statement	8. Makes closing statement

You can toss a coin to decide which team will go first, and you can determine the length of each segment of the debate as a class. You may wish to assign specific duties to your teammates, such as team captain, notetaker, main argument presenters, counterargument presenters, and so on. Notes on what both sides say during the debate will be very useful to you later when you write your essay for this chapter.

PART 2	# Language for Writing

Discussing Energy

1 The following words are useful when writing about energy. Some of them have been used in this chapter. Make sure you know the meaning of each. Add other words you have learned in this chapter on the lines at the end of each column.

Adjectives	Nouns	Verbs
mechanical	heat	release
chemical	source	store
electrical	conservation	burn
atomic	matter	use
solar	friction	absorb
nuclear	panel	produce
energy-efficient	watt	change
photovoltaic	silicon	convert
flexible	power	generate
_____	breakthrough	_____
_____	cell	_____
_____	utilities	_____
	_____	
	_____	
	_____	

Describing How Things Work

The words and expressions below will help you describe the processes of simple and complex machines. The following expressions are used to describe parts or components. X represents the machine, or the object.

$$\text{Xs} \begin{cases} \text{are} \\ \text{involve} \\ \text{include} \\ \text{must have} \\ \text{are provided with} \end{cases}$$

Example

All solar water heaters *involve* a large, black, flat area that receives the solar radiation and heats the water.

The following expressions can describe the position of an object.

$$\text{X is} \begin{cases} \text{faced} \\ \text{positioned} \\ \text{tilted} \\ \text{pointed} \end{cases}$$

Example

The absorber is *faced* south and *tilted* at a 40-degree angle with the horizontal.

Note that the expressions used to describe position are all in the passive voice. The passive voice is used frequently in scientific writing. Descriptions of processes for machines or objects almost always use the passive voice. Review the form of the passive below and read the examples that describe processes.

Passive: BE + past participle (verb + *ed*)

Examples

Solar water heaters *are provided* with glass or plastic covers.

The absorbing unit *is placed* in an insulated box.

Solar water heaters of different kinds *are shown* in the following diagrams.

2 Write a paragraph in which you describe the parts, position, and processes of a solar cell. Compare your paragraph to a classmate's.

3 Write a paragraph about the breakthrough you researched in Part 1. Include as many words from this section as you consider appropriate.

4   Choose one of the following items and describe how it works and what it does. You
may want to draw a diagram to accompany your explanation.

a light bulb

a water wheel

a gas stove

PART 3 # Systems for Writing

Processes

Review Points

- An effective way to make a point in an essay is to show cause-effect relationships between events or ideas.
- There are several ways to organize a cause-effect essay.

New Points

- Writing that describes processes (often in scientific writing) requires careful organization.
- Chronological descriptions of processes use signals such as *first, second, next,* and *finally* to describe the steps the process involves.
- Structural descriptions of processes describe and/or analyze an object or event to determine the organization.
- The thesis statement in a process essay is often an announcement of what you are going to describe and how you will go about it.

Read this example of a process paragraph that contains a chronological description.

There are several steps to follow in order to write a good essay in class. First, the writer must read the assignment very carefully and make sure he or she understands the topic. Second, the writer should jot down ideas that come to mind when thinking about the topic. Next, the writer should organize the notes and compose a thesis statement. The writer should plan how much time he or she should spend on each part of the essay and stick to the schedule carefully. Finally, after the essay is written, the writer must proofread carefully to catch mistakes.

Now read this example of a process paragraph that contains a structural description.

A solar cooker is made with plastic on a hoop laid over a parabolic concrete mound. It is lined with a mosaic of one-inch mirrors. The adjustable U-frame made of water pipe rotates around a pipe driven into the ground, and the reflecting shell is suspended from the horizontal pipe that supports the small circular grill for holding the cooking vessel. The frame is rotated, and the reflecting solar collector is tilted to bring the shadow of the kettle to the center of the collector by pulling a chain that can be caught over a protruding bolt in the frame.*

*Adapted from Daniels Farrington, *Direct Use of the Sun's Energy,* New York: Ballantine Books.

1   A friend of yours is coming to this country. As soon as he arrives, he will call you from the airport. He has never used a public telephone here so you want to write him and give him instructions. In a paragraph, describe the steps your friend should follow in order to complete his call. Exchange paragraphs with a partner and choose the clearest explanation.

2   In a paragraph, describe one of the following mechanisms, including its parts, the position of its parts, and how it is used.

- a pulley
- a mechanical pencil
- a pair of scissors
- an eyedropper

3   Describe a process that you are familiar with. It can be scientific or nonscientific. You might consider some of the following: writing an essay, looking for a place to live, preparing a holiday meal, doing the laundry, getting cash from an ATM. Read your paragraph to the class.

4   In a paragraph, describe the parts of a device or machine that you are familiar with, their positions, and how the device or machine operates.

Focus on Testing

Considering the Audience

Activity 1 asks you to write something for a friend. When writing an essay under time pressure, read the directions carefully to determine who you are writing for. This will tell you how formal or informal your writing should be.

Writing Assignments

Write an essay on one of the following topics. Use the ideas you've discussed and the material you've written so far in this chapter as the basis of your essay.

1. Expand writing you did on a breakthrough in solar energy into an essay. Choose an activity that you spent time on and that interested you.

2. Choose one source of energy and describe its advantages. Include in your discussion a description of how the particular energy source works.

3. Discuss the advantages and disadvantages of solar power. Include in your discussion a description of how it works.

4. Explain, agree with, or disagree with the following quotation:

Almost all the energy on earth originated in the sun.
                                     —*Compton's Encyclopedia*

5. Write an essay on any aspect of solar power or alternative energy that interests you.

PART 4	# Evaluating for Rewriting

Evaluating the First Draft

Step 1

Choose a partner and exchange your essays. Read your partner's first draft to get the general idea; don't focus on specific details or on grammar or punctuation. Use the following questions to evaluate each other's essays.

1. What is the main idea?

_____

_____

2. What is the writer's purpose in writing this essay?

_____

_____

3. Did the writer accomplish what he or she set out to do?

   Yes _____   No _____

4. Do you have any suggestions for improving this first draft?

_____

_____

Step 2

Return each other's essays. Read your partner's evaluation. Discuss any questions you have with your partner.

Step 3

Now write a second draft, considering your partner's evaluation comments.

Evaluating the Second Draft

Step 1

Exchange your second drafts. Use the following questions to evaluate your partner's essay.

1. Read the thesis statement. Predict what you expect the writer to describe and how you expect the essay to be developed.

    _____

    _____

2. Does the writer describe a process?

    Yes _____   No _____

3. If the answer is yes, what type of process is it?

    _____

    _____

4. Does the essay include a description of parts and position?

    Yes _____   No _____

    If not, and if you feel that the writer should include these descriptions, make suggestions for improvement.

    _____

    _____

5. Is the process clearly described?

    Yes _____   No _____

    If your answer is no, make suggestions for improvement.

    _____

    _____

6. How many words and expressions from Part 2, Language for Writing, did the writer use in this essay?

   _____

7. Were they used correctly in terms of both meaning and grammar?

   Yes _____   No _____

8. Do you have any suggestions for your partner's future work?

   _____

   _____

9. What are the strengths of this essay?

   _____

   _____

Step 2

Return your second drafts. Read your partner's evaluation. Discuss any questions you have with your partner.

Writing the Final Draft

Now write a final draft, considering your partner's comments. Turn in this draft to your teacher.

Video Activities: Advances in Medicine

Before You Watch.   Discuss these questions in small groups.

1. What do you think happens if the nerves that control your muscles die? Do you know the name of the disease that kills these nerves?
2. Have you ever known anyone who had a disease that affected his or her movement? How did this disease affect his/her life?

Watch.   Circle the correct answers.

1. The main idea of this video segment is that _____.

   a. ALS is a very difficult disease to have

   b. a cure will soon be found for ALS

   c. there is hope for people with ALS

2. Jerry Lineberger controls his wheelchair and his computer by moving his
   _____.

   a. legs and arms   b. hands and feet   c. head and eyes

3. Dr. Jeffrey Rosenfeld's treatment _____.

   a. has cured some people

   b. may help some people live longer

   c. is dangerous and difficult

Watch Again.   Write answers to these questions.

1. How long has Jerry Lineberger had ALS?

   _____

2. What are the initials of the protein that Dr. Rosenfeld uses in his
   treatment?

   _____

3. Use the words below to complete the description of Dr. Rosenfeld's
   treatment.

abdomen	catheter	implanted	inserted
pump	release	spinal fluid	vertebra

A _____ the size of a hockey puck is _____ in the

_____. A _____ is _____ between two

_____. Tiny holes continuously _____ the drug into

the _____.

4. *Diagnosed* is a verb. The noun is _____.

5. *Optimistically* is an adverb. The adjective is _____.

6. Listen and write words that have these meanings.

   a. incredible   _____

   b. a doctor who specializes in the nervous system   _____

   c. to increase the amount of time   _____

   d. unproved theory   _____

After You Watch.   Write an essay about another medical treatment that you
know about. Explain how the treatment works, how effective it is, and if it has
any negative side effects.

Chapter 9

Art and Entertainment

IN THIS CHAPTER

You will gather information and write about an aspect of art.

Ideas for Writing

Getting Started

1 Study the following works of art and answer the questions about them in small groups.

1. Calypso Mural in Trinidad, Spain, twentieth century

2. Guardian figure, Gabon, nineteenth century

3. Cave painting, Spain, 13,000 B.C.

4. *The Seven Pines,* Tang Tse-Hua, China, fourteenth century

5. Prayer rug, Persia, eighteenth century

6. *Guernica,* Pablo Picasso, Spain, 1938

7. Parisian scene, Robert Doisneau, photographer, 1930s

1. What do you think the artist's purpose was in creating each work of art? In other words, what do you think its intended *function* was? Some possible functions for art are for use in religion, to tell a story, to educate, to give pleasure. Try to think of other functions.

   _____

   _____

   _____

   _____

   _____

   _____

   _____

2. How does each work of art represent the *values* of the culture that produced it? That is, how does it show what is important in that culture?

   _____

   _____

   _____

   _____

   _____

   _____

   _____

3. Does the work have a message? What is it? What elements (or parts) of the work communicate this message?

   _____

   _____

   _____

   _____

   _____

   _____

   _____

4. Which of these works of art do you like? Why?

_____

_____

_____

_____

_____

_____

_____

_____

2   In small groups, name some other well-known works of art. Discuss their functions, the cultural values they represent, and their messages.

Reading for Ideas

3   The following passage, "African Art as Nonverbal Communication," is by Thelma R. Newman, a specialist in African art and culture. In this passage, she discusses the essential qualities of African art and explains how these qualities relate to African cultural values. Before you read, answer the following questions in small groups.

Prereading Questions

1. What is art, in your opinion? In other words, how do you define the word *art*?

_____

_____

2. Are you familiar with African art? What are some different forms of African art? Share your knowledge with the class.

_____

_____

3. Describe the African art at the beginning of the chapter (the guardian figure from Gabon). Can you guess what its function might be?

_____

_____

African Art as Nonverbal Communication

The word *art* is not relevant when we describe African "art," because it is really a European term. It first grew out of Greek philosophy and was later reinforced by European culture. The use of other terms, such as exotic art, primitive art, *art sauvage,* and so on, to distinguish Western art from non-West-
5 ern art is just as misleading. Most of these terms are pejorative; they imply that African art is on a lower cultural level. Levels of culture are irrelevant here, since African and European attitudes toward the creative act are so different. Since there is no term in our language to distinguish between the essential differences in thinking, it is best then to describe standards of African art.

10 *African art is functional.* Its function is its purpose, whether it is economic, magical, or religious. There is, though, some art for its own sake, such as in the embellishment of pulleys used in weaving. The carving on the pulley may not make for a stronger pulley (a metal hook would be cheaper and stronger), but when asked why another kind wasn't used, the weaver answered, "One does not
15 want to live without pretty things."

African art is a way of experiencing the world. All its forms, whether masks, sculpture, houses, fabrics, pottery, poetry, music, or dance, make the invisible visible and reveal the meaning of the confrontation between life and death. (It was Paul Klee, influenced by African art, who said that the task of art was to
20 make the invisible visible.)

The African artist works from the force to the form that embodies it. Until the twentieth century, European artists, inspired by Greek traditions, started from a concrete form, usually that of the human figure, to express the divine. The African artist, however, begins with a sense of a spiritual presence inside him,
25 which he then expresses through art, in a concrete form.

The African artist is not considered an artist. He may be a farmer who carves or a smith who has magical powers. The responsibility for understanding the operation of forces that come from the divine power, and of controlling them in a meaningful way, lies in the medicine man or priest. It is the priest who com-
30 municates the need for a certain form to the carver if it is to be a spiritual object. (That is why carvers don't see anything wrong in copying another carver's work. Copying is just another form of flattery.)

The African conception of art is a communal conception as compared with European individualistic expression. To the African, community existed before
35 the individual existed, and the individual is just a small part of a long tradition. The sense of unity extends to nature and to the earth—the earth belongs to ancestors.

Secret societies, supporting the medicine man, maintain standards of behavior by special initiation tests, rituals for many occasions, oaths of secrecy,
40 and the like. They supervise morality, uphold tribal traditions, and dispense justice. They set standards for art forms from birth through puberty, marriage, and death. Masks, sculptures in the form of ancestor figures, fetishes, and ritual implements (rattles and drums) follow these traditions. Fetishes are objects that have magical powers for a special purpose and are usually crudely fashioned
45 by the medicine man.

African mask,
Ivory Coast, early
twentieth century

African art gives form to the supernatural and invisible. African art is necessarily abstract; it does not even attempt to imitate concrete appearances. How does one represent the power and virtue of an ancestor or the rhythm of an animal concretely? From this comes unity and the reduction of every formal
50 element to its eternal form.

African art is in equilibrium with nature and forms a communion with nature. To the African, sculpture can be a receptacle for an ancestor's spirituality and has the ability to transmit that spirituality when necessary. Its message or meaning becomes its presence.

55 *African art is closer to life than the art of other countries. Its art forms are within every person's reach.* They are a necessity, an integral force, and part of living. As functional forms, they invite direct participation in their uses. This is the vitality of African art.

In summary, African art explains the past, describes values and a way of
60 life, helps people relate to supernatural forces, mediates their social relations, expresses emotions, and enhances people's lives as an embellishment denoting pride or status as well as providing entertainment (such as with dance and music).

Postreading Questions

4   Answer these questions.

1. Why does the author reject the terms "exotic art," "primitive art," and *"art sauvage"* for describing African art?

2. Summarize in your own words the nine characteristics of African art that Newman describes. Compare these characteristics of African art with those of the art of your country or culture.

3. How is copying another artist's work regarded in African cultures, according to Newman? How is copying another's artistic creation regarded in your culture (or another culture that you are familiar with)? Explain.

Thinking Critically

Applying What You've Learned

Applying new concepts to a familiar situation helps you understand them more fully. Practice this by applying what you've learned about African art to the art of your country or culture. Work in small groups and answer these questions about your culture:

■ Is art primarily functional?

■ Are artists in your country considered to be "special" people?

■ Is the production of art in your culture a communal effort or an individual one?

■ Are there set standards for art in your culture?

■ Does art in your country deal primarily with religion or spirituality?

■ Is art a large part of everyday life in your country?

Freewriting

5   Choose one of the works of art depicted in this chapter, or a different one, and discuss its function and the cultural values it represents. Say whether or not you like the work and why. Write for twenty minutes.

Gathering Information

6   Get more information about one of the aspects of art discussed in this chapter. Choose one of the following:

■ a particular artist (for example, Picasso)

■ a particular work of art (for example, the *Mona Lisa*)

■ a function of art (for example, to express a religious belief)

■ a particular culture's artistic traditions (for example, Native American)

Get as much information as you can by doing Web or library research. Write a one- to three-page summary of the information. Make copies of the works of art to support your information.

7   Share your findings from the preceding activity with your classmates. Present your research in small groups or to the entire class. Make sure you bring copies of the artwork to show your classmates.

Your presentation should take five to ten minutes. Organize it as you do an essay, with an introduction, a body, and a conclusion. As you listen to the other presentations, take notes, because you may be able to use the information in your writing assignment for this chapter.

| **PART 2** | # Language for Writing |

Analyzing and Describing Art

Writers use specialized terms and expressions when they discuss and write about art. Newman's article on African art contains some of these. Some you may already know and others may be new to you.

1   Find out how many words and expressions related to art you already know. To do this, work in small groups and select six pictures of works of art from the beginning of this chapter or from your research. Look at the pictures one at a time and write any words or expressions that come into your mind. When you finish listing words, organize related words into categories that your group agrees on. Sample categories are **Color**, **Shape**, and **Function**.

Example

Persian prayer rug

Color	**Shape**	**Function**
rust red	geometric	spiritual
dark blues		

Decide with your teacher which words and expressions may be the most useful in your writing and keep a copy of these for later.

2   Find and underline in Newman's article each of the following expressions about the functions of art. Make sure you understand what each expression means and how it is used.

art
that
{
is a response to something
is functional
reveals the meaning of something
conforms to a tradition
represents or symbolizes something
transmits an idea or feeling
art for its own sake
art for communal/individualistic expression
}

3   Here are some additional words and expressions for describing art itself, as opposed to its functions. Newman uses some of them in her article. With a partner, discuss what each word means.

composition	still life	figure
subject	landscape	portrait
model	sculpture	photography
realistic	surrealistic	

4 Describe each of the photos of works of art in Part 1 on pages 152–153. Use as many of the words and expressions from the preceding lists as you can.

5 Write sentences in which you give an example of at least eight of the expressions from the preceding lists. Use the pictures or your research in Part 1 or both. Make sure that each example sentence defines the term. For example: "The carvings on pulleys in certain parts of Africa are an example of art that is functional."

6 Write a paragraph in which you describe and analyze a piece of art in terms of function or cultural values or both. You can select one that you've already discussed or you can find another work of art. Use words and expressions from this section, including some from your group discussion. Include a picture of the work of art with your paragraph if possible.

7 Rewrite your Freewriting activity from Part 1. Use words and expressions from this section.

PART 3   # Systems for Writing

Introductions and Conclusions

> **Review Points**
> - An academic essay contains an introduction with a thesis statement, body paragraphs, and a conclusion.
> - Common introduction types include general-to-specific, chronological, and problem-solution.
> - A common conclusion type is one that restates or summarizes the main points of the essay.

Introductions

> **New Points**
> - An introduction in an academic essay prepares readers for what is to come and draws them into your essay.
> - An introduction should create a high level of interest.
> - Essay introductions that create a high level of interest are those that begin with *background information*, a *quotation*, a *definition*, or a *summary*.

Read the following descriptions and examples of these four types of introductions:

1. *Background information.* Presents background on the topic that slowly leads up to the thesis. For example:

> Over the past fifty years, the concept of success for many Chinese women has changed dramatically. Earlier in this century, a woman was successful if she was a respectful daughter-in-law, a dutiful wife, and a responsible mother. That is, a successful woman was one who did what her mother-in-law wished, kept a clean house, and took very good care of her children. However, success today for a Chinese woman has a different meaning. Now success means working outside the home and achieving a status in society equal to that of men.

2. *Quotation.* Must be directly related to the main idea of the essay; it can be from reading that you have done to prepare for your essay or it can be from a well-known saying, an appropriate remark from a famous person, or a line from a song or a poem. For example:

> In an effort to create the right environment for students, educators constantly propose new ways to educate students. Some people, such as William O'Connor, insist: "We have no inferior education in our schools; what we have been getting is an inferior type of student." However, it is wrong to say that it is only the student who is inferior, not the school. One system is not appropriate for all students. Problems arise when students' individual needs are not met. Therefore, the needs of the students must be considered when deciding which system is best. Basically, there are three types of systems that are right for different students: an authoritarian system, a free system, and a combination of the two.

3. *Definition.* Prepares the reader for applications and examples of the concept or term being defined. For example:

> *Success* is a term that has many meanings. For students, success can mean getting good grades or getting a good job after graduation. To a businessperson, success is making a lot of money and gaining a position of power. To an artist, however, success is having the ability to express inner feelings and having people recognize the artist's intentions.

4. *Summary.* Summarizes a reading selection (or a lecture or speech) and prepares the reader for an analysis or discussion of what has been summarized. For example:

> In her article "African Art as Nonverbal Communication," Thelma Newman discusses African art and the inadequacy of European attempts to categorize it. Newman describes several characteristics common to most examples of African art and shows how these characteristics reveal a great deal about African culture. It is clear, therefore, that one can learn about the customs and values of a country by studying its art.

1 Rewrite four introductions from previous essays that you have written in this course. Use each of the four types of introductions described in this section. Exchange your new introductions with a partner and evaluate each other's work.

Conclusions

New Points

■ A good conclusion makes the reader feel that you have fulfilled the promise of your thesis statement and that you are effectively bringing your essay to a close.

■ One type of conclusion that effectively brings an essay to a close and leaves the reader with a challenging or provocative thought on the topic is one that restates the main points of the essay and includes some new information on the topic.

■ The new information in this kind of conclusion can be a statement, a question, or your opinion about the essay topic (unless you've already expressed it elsewhere in the essay).

The following is an example of an effective conclusion. It is from the student essay "The Nature of a Realistic Person," pages 13 and 14, Chapter 1. Notice that in this conclusion the writer restates the main points of the essay and includes new information on the topic to challenge the reader.

> By now it should be clear why being objective, critical, and rational is what distinguishes the realist from the dreamer and the neurotic. It is also clear that being realistic is a very desirable trait. Not only that, at this point it can be stated that the realist is the model of a well-balanced individual.

Focus on Testing

Having a Repertoire of Introductions and Conclusions

Part 3 presents new ways to write introductions and conclusions. Having a repertoire (a collection) of two or three introduction and conclusion types will help you plan and write more quickly in test-taking situations.

 **2** Find a conclusion from one of your previous essays that did not contain new information or ideas. Rewrite it so that it *does* contain new information or ideas. Exchange your rewritten conclusion with a partner for evaluation.

Writing Assignments

Write an essay on one of the following topics. Use the ideas you've discussed and written about so far in this chapter and previous chapters as the basis for your essay. Use one of the four new types of introductions and a conclusion that contains new information or ideas.

1. Analyze the functions of a particular work of art. You may wish to use one of those discussed in Part 1 of this chapter or you may wish to choose a new one.

2. Draw a connection between two or three of the most important values in your culture and the art of your culture. In other words, show how the art of your culture represents the values of your culture, as Newman has done with African art.

3. Explain Paul Klee's statement that the task of art is to make the invisible visible. Use well-known works of art as examples.

4. Is film art? What about photography? Choose one of these and explain your answer in terms of cultural values and the functions of art.

5. Explain, agree with, or disagree with the following quotation:

   Good painting is like good cooking: It can be tasted, but not explained.
   —Maurice de Vlaminck

6. Write an essay in which you react to something you've read about art, either the passage in this chapter or the reading you did for the Gathering Information section. Make sure you summarize the reading in your introduction.

7. Write about any aspect of art that interests you.

| PART 4 | # Evaluating for Rewriting |

Evaluating the First Draft

Step 1

Choose a partner and exchange your essays. Read your partner's first draft to get the general idea; don't focus on specific details or on grammar or punctuation. Use the following questions to evaluate each other's essays.

1. What is the main idea?

    _____

    _____

2. What is the writer's purpose in writing this essay?

    _____

    _____

3. Did the writer accomplish what he or she set out to do?

    Yes _____   No _____

4. Do you have any suggestions for improving this first draft?

    _____

    _____

    _____

    _____

Step 2

Return each other's essays. Read your partner's evaluation. Discuss any questions you have with your partner.

Step 3

Now write a second draft, considering your partner's evaluation comments.

Evaluating the Second Draft

Step 1

Exchange your second drafts. Use the questions here and on the next page to evaluate your partner's essay.

1. Read the introductory paragraph. What technique has the writer used in the introduction?

   _____

   _____

2. How effective is the introduction? Does it make you want to read more? Does it lead into the thesis statement?

   _____

   _____

   _____

   _____

   If the introduction is not as effective as it could be, make suggestions for improvement.

   _____

   _____

   _____

   _____

3. Read the rest of the essay. Does the introductory paragraph prepare you for the essay as a whole? Explain.

   _____

   _____

4. Now read the conclusion. Is it simply a restatement of the writer's thesis or does it include some new information?

   _____

   _____

   If it is simply a restatement, suggest how new information might be added. If it contains new information, is the information provocative or challenging to you?

   Yes _____   No _____

If not, make suggestions for improvement.

_____

_____

_____

_____

5. Did the writer use words and expressions from Part 2, Language for Writing, in this essay? Give some examples:

_____

_____

_____

6. Did the writer use them correctly?

Yes _____   No _____

7. Do you have any suggestions for the writer in future work?

_____

_____

_____

8. What did you particularly like about this essay?

_____

_____

_____

Step 2

Return your second drafts. Read your partner's evaluation. Discuss any questions you have with your partner.

Writing the Final Draft

Now write a final draft, considering your partner's comments. Turn in this draft to your teacher.

Video Activities: Women in Jazz

Before You Watch.   Discuss these questions in small groups.

1. Which of these musicians played jazz?

    a. Billie Holiday   b. the Beatles   c. Luciano Pavarotti

2. Do you ever listen to jazz? Do you know any other famous jazz musicians?

Watch.   Circle the correct answers.

1. What kind of music does Rosetta Records publish?

    a. songs by modern female jazz musicians

    b. songs from early jazz musicians

    c. early songs by female jazz musicians

2. According to Rosetta Weitz most people today do not realize that women _____.

    a. sang with jazz bands

    b. had a powerful influence on jazz

    c. were better jazz musicians than men

3. Successful female jazz musicians had _____.

    a. wealth and power

    b. everything but power

    c. to depend on men

4. What did early female jazz singers sing about?

    a. love   d. abandonment

    b. war   e. poverty

    c. pride

Watch Again.   Answer these questions in small groups.

1. Complete the names of these jazz musicians. Put a check mark (✔) next to the women.

Jazz Musicians	Women?
a. _____Cox	_____
b. _____McKinney	_____
c. Maxine_____	_____
d. Lester _____	_____
e. _____Calloway	_____
f. _____Ellington	_____
g. _____Basie	_____
h. _____Humes	_____

2. *Impact* means the same as _____.
   a. destruction   b. influence   c. connection

3. Something that is *quintessential* is _____.
   a. a perfect example   b. necessary   c. successful

4. *Alongside* means the same as _____.
   a. near   b. with   c. instead of

After You Watch.   Use information from the video segment and the chapter to write about how music is similar to or different from the visual arts such as painting, sculpture, and photography.

Chapter 10

Conflict and Reconciliation

IN THIS CHAPTER

You will read and talk about different conflicts and solutions and write a proposal for a reconciliation effort.

PART 1

Ideas for Writing

Getting Started

1   It is not difficult to find conflicts around us. They exist between individuals, groups, and nations for many different reasons. Look at the photo on page 169 and at the following photos. What conflict does each show? Work in small groups to complete the chart that follows.

1. International organization that promotes wildlife and environmental protection

2. People protesting animal research

3. People protesting military spending

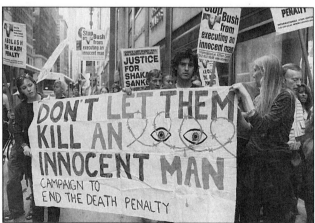

4. Protest against the death penalty

Photo	What is the conflict?	Who is it between	What is one solution?
1	Protection of animals and the environment vs. development	Environmentalist vs. people who support business, residential development	Limit development

Reading for Ideas

2 Gary Snyder is a well-known American poet who was born in San Francisco in 1930. His opinions are largely based on his studies of Eastern philosophy and the spiritual beliefs of Native Americans. The following selections (a speech and a poem) are from his book *Turtle Island*. Discuss the following questions in small groups before you read.

Prereading Questions

1. Review the meanings of these words:

wilderness	constituency	chamber
humanism	sphere	ecological
millennium	ecosystem	

2. Do you think governments should protect and preserve wilderness areas?

   _____

   _____

3. What can we learn from nature?

   _____

   _____

Turtle Island (Selections)

I.

I am a poet. My teachers are other poets, American Indians, and a few Buddhist priests in Japan. The reason I am here is because I wish to bring a voice from the wilderness, my constituency. I wish to be a spokesman for a realm that is not usually represented either in intellectual chambers or in the chambers
5 of government.

I would like to think of a new definition of humanism and a new definition of democracy that would include the nonhuman, that would have representation from those spheres. This is what I think we mean by an ecological conscience.

I don't like Western culture because I think it has much in it that is inherently
10 wrong and that is at the root of the environmental crisis that is not recent; it is very ancient; it has been building up for a millennium. There are many things in Western culture that are admirable. But a culture that alienates itself from the very ground of its own being—from the wilderness outside (that is to say, wild nature, the wild, self-contained, self-informing, ecosystems) and from that other
15 wilderness, the wilderness within—is doomed to a very destructive behavior, ultimately perhaps self-destructive behavior.

The West is not the only culture that carries these destructive seeds. China had effectively deforested itself by A.D. 800. The soils of the Middle East were ruined even earlier. The forests that once covered the mountains of Yugoslavia
20 were stripped to build the Roman fleet, and those mountains have looked like Utah ever since. The soils of southern Italy and Sicily were ruined by slave-labor farming in the Roman Empire. The soils of the Atlantic seaboard in the United States were effectively ruined before the American Revolution because of the one-crop (tobacco) farming. So the same forces have been at work in East and
25 West.

A line is drawn between primitive peoples and civilized peoples. I think there is a wisdom in the world view of primitive peoples that we have to refer ourselves to, and learn from. If we are on the verge of postcivilization, then our next step must take account of the primitive world view which has traditionally
30 and intelligently tried to keep open lines of communication with the forces of nature. You cannot communicate with the forces of nature in a laboratory. One of the problems is that we simply do not know much about primitive people and primitive cultures. If we can tentatively accommodate the possibility that nature has a degree of authenticity and intelligence that requires that we look at it more
35 sensitively, then we can move on to the next step.

II. For the Children

The rising hills, the slopes,
of statistics
lie before us.
the steep climb
40 of everything, going up,
up, as we all
go down.
In the next century
or the one beyond that,
45 they say,
are valleys, pastures,
we can meet there in peace
if we make it.
To climb these coming crests
50 one word to you, to
you and your children:
stay together
learn the flowers
go light

—Gary Snyder

Postreading Questions

3 Answer these questions.

1. What is Snyder's constituency?

    _____

    _____

2. Write this sentence from Snyder's speech in your words: "I wish to be a
    spokesman for a realm that is not usually represented either in intellectual
    chambers or in the chambers of government."

    _____

    _____

3. In his speech, what conflict does Snyder discuss? Who is it between?

    _____

    _____

4. In "For the Children," Snyder offers hope for reconciliation of the conflict. What advice does he give for helping this reconciliation to happen?

_____

_____

5. According to Snyder, what is one thing that is wrong with Western culture?

_____

_____

6. What can "primitive" peoples teach us?

_____

_____

Thinking Critically

Interpreting Metaphors

A metaphor is a word or phrase that describes something by comparing it to something else without using the words *like* or *as*. Many writers use metaphors. In "For the Children," Snyder compares elements of nature to information. He writes:

_____

The rising hills, the slopes,
of statistics
lie before us.

_____

In small groups, read this poem again. What do the words *hills* and *valleys* represent? Share your ideas and discuss the reasons for your interpretations. There are no right or wrong answers—many interpretations are possible.

Freewriting

4   Write for twenty minutes without stopping about a conflict that interests you. Describe the different sides of the issue and propose one or more solutions.

Gathering Information

5 Each of your classmates will share the conflicts they wrote about in Freewriting. Take notes on six of the conflicts they describe in the following chart:

What is the conflict?	Who is it between?	What is one solution?

6 Fire Mountain is a small community in the southwestern United States. Read the following passage, which describes a conflict the residents are trying to resolve.

> Fire Mountain is a scenic area that attracts many hikers and tourists every year. It is famous for its ancient Native American dwellings and varied wildlife. Fire Mountain also contains a rich supply of coal. Winters are cold, so the people near Fire Mountain need an inexpensive and steady supply of fuel, which Fire Mountain could provide. In addition, there is a high unemployment rate in the area. If Fire Mountain were mined for coal, people could get work. The problem is that strip-mining makes the land ugly and kills animals. How should the people at Fire Mountain solve this problem?

Work in small groups to propose a solution to the problem. Try to reach a consensus in your group, then present it to the class.

| PART 2 | # Language for Writing |

Using Abstract Nouns

Abstract nouns—nouns that refer to ideas or concepts rather than to physical objects—are useful when you are writing about social responsibility. The following list includes many of the abstract nouns from Snyder's speech and poem. Read the list. Then do the following activities.

humanism	authenticity	conscience	space
wisdom	responsibility	peace	society
advice	morality	freedom	nature

1   First, choose eight of the words and write definitions of them.

Word   **Meaning**

_____   _____

_____   _____

_____   _____

_____   _____

_____   _____

_____   _____

_____   _____

_____   _____

2   Now use five nouns from your list in sentences that relate to a conflict. Choose words that are new to you. Write your words and sentences in the following chart.

Word	Sentence

Giving Definitions

The assignments in this chapter require you to write definitions. Review the following expressions, which will help you incorporate definitions into your writing.

$$X \left\{ \begin{array}{l} \text{is} \\ \text{means} \\ \text{refers to} \\ \text{is considered to be} \end{array} \right\} Y$$

3   Develop your Freewrite into a paragraph. Include as many abstract nouns from this section as you can.

4   In a paragraph, write about the conflict Snyder describes.

PART 3   # Systems for Writing

Definitions: Literal and Stipulated

Review Points

- In addition to general-to-specific, chronological, and problem-solution introductions, there are background information, quotation, definition, and summary introductions.
- The levels of specificity of ideas in a conclusion often go from specific to general.

New Points

- It is sometimes necessary or useful to define a word or expression in an essay. Two types of definitions are the literal, or dictionary, definition and a stipulated, or particular, definition.
- Literal definitions in a single sentence clarify the meaning of a term as it is generally defined.
- Stipulated definitions explain the meaning of a word in a particular context.

Look at these examples of literal definitions.

■ Morality is rightness or pureness of behavior, or of an action.

■ Intelligence means an ability to learn and understand.

Look at these examples of stipulated definitions.

■ The character's behavior in this story exhibited morality. He demonstrated his loyalty to other humans and he was aware of the risks involved.

■ Our company defines intelligence as the ability to grasp new information quickly and put it to use efficiently.

1   Look back at Snyder's speech on page 172. First write literal definitions of each of the following words. Then write definitions that explain Snyder's interpretation of these expressions. These are stipulated definitions.

Term	Literal Definition	Stipulated Definition
seeds		
teacher		
humanism		

Focus on Testing

Brainstorming to Get Started

Sometimes it is difficult to get started writing when you are under pressure. By quickly jotting down any ideas you have about the topic, you can overcome temporary writer's block. Brainstorming helps you collect vocabulary and gather knowledge.

2 Choose one of the photos on page 170. What conflict does it represent? Write about this conflict and a possible resolution in a paragraph.

3 Write a stipulated definition for one of the words below.

loyalty	morality
peace	education
brotherhood	

4 Write a paragraph about a person you admire for his or her work in resolving a conflict.

Writing Assignments

Write an essay on at least one of the following topics. Use the ideas you've discussed and the material you've written so far in this chapter and previous chapters as the basis for your essay. Try to include a stipulated definition in your essay.

1. Choose a current conflict that interests you. Write an essay in which you explain the conflict and propose a resolution. Refer to work you have done in previous chapters.

2. Write about a conflict that varies from culture to culture. For example, young people preparing to get married run into difficulties, but these difficulties are very different across cultures. Compare the same conflict in two cultures.

3. Many consider the following people heroes because of their contributions to resolving important conflicts. Develop an essay around one or more of these people by describing the conflict and explaining how the person helped reach a resolution.

Mohandas Gandhi	Martin Luther King, Jr.
Anwar Sadat	Mao Zedong
Mother Teresa	Rigoberta Menchu

4. Explain, agree with, or disagree with the following quotation:

    There can be hope only for a society which acts as one big family, and not as many little ones.

    —Anwar Sadat

    ---

5. Write about a song that proposes a solution to a conflict.

6. Write an essay about any aspect of conflict and reconciliation that interests you.

| **PART 4** | # Evaluating for Rewriting |

Evaluating the First Draft

Step 1

Choose a partner and exchange your essays. Read your partner's first draft to get the general idea; don't focus on specific details or on grammar or punctuation. Use the following questions to evaluate each other's essays.

1. What is the main idea?

    _____

    _____

2. What is the writer's purpose in writing this essay?

    _____

    _____

3. Did the writer accomplish what he or she set out to do?

    Yes _____   No _____

4. Do you have any suggestions for improving this first draft?

    _____

    _____

Step 2

Return each other's essays. Read your partner's evaluation. Discuss any questions you have with your partner.

Step 3

Now write a second draft, considering your partner's evaluation comments.

Evaluating the Second Draft

Step 1

Exchange your second drafts. Use the following questions to evaluate your partner's essay.

1. What parts of this essay did you like?

   _____

   _____

2. Does the writer include definitions in this essay?

   _____

   _____

   a. How many of these are literal definitions?

   b. How many are stipulated definitions?

3. Are the definitions easy to understand?

   Yes _____   No _____

   If not, make suggestions for improvement.

   _____

   _____

4. If the writer uses words and expressions from Part 2, Language for Writing, are they used correctly?

   Yes _____   No _____

5. Do you have any suggestions for improving this essay?

   _____

   _____

Step 2

Return your second drafts. Read your partner's evaluation. Discuss any questions you have with your partner.

Writing the Final Draft

Now write a final draft, considering your partner's comments. Turn in this draft to your teacher.

Video Activities: A Strike

Before You Watch.   Discuss these questions in small groups.

1. Why do workers go on strike?

2. Are government workers allowed to go on strike?

Watch.   Circle the correct answers.

1. What have the unionized workers of the county of Los Angeles decided
    to do?

    a. go back to work   b. go on strike   c. go to court

2. How much of a pay increase is the union asking for?

    a. 15.5% over three years   b. 15% over two years   c. 5% in one year

3. How much of a pay increase is the county offering the union?

    a. 19% over 5 years   b. 9% over three years   c. 11% over two years

Watch Again.   Answer these questions in small groups.

1. Check the employees that are mentioned in the video segment.

    a. _____ librarians   e. _____ cooks

    b. _____ nurses   f. _____ typists

    c. _____ building maintenance workers   g. _____ cashiers

    d. _____ teachers

2. Which of the employees above are going back to work tomorrow?

    _____

3. According to the woman in the video, which two of these problems do
    the nurses have?

    a. too little pay   b. too much work   c. poor working conditions

4. *Principal* means _____.

    a. the most important   b. the smallest   c. the leader

5. When something is *booming*, it is _____.

    a. just starting   b. growing rapidly   c. declining

6. If something is *critical*, it is _____.

    a. dangerous   b. expensive   c. necessary

After You Watch.   Write an essay about unions. What are the advantages and
disadvantages to belonging to a union? How do they help society? What would
happen if there were no unions? What would happen if unions had too much
power?

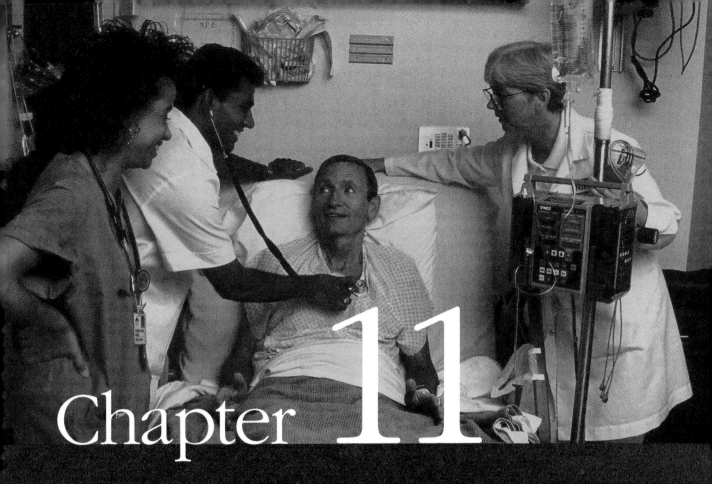

Chapter 11

Medicine and Science

IN THIS CHAPTER

You will do research on a healing practice and write about an aspect of medicine and healing that interests you.

PART 1 **Ideas for Writing**

Getting Started

1   Study these pictures of various healing practices and answer the questions that
follow.

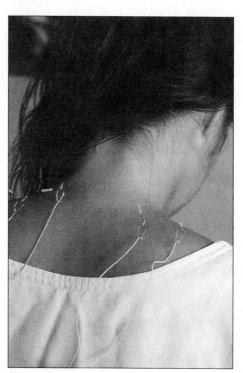

1.

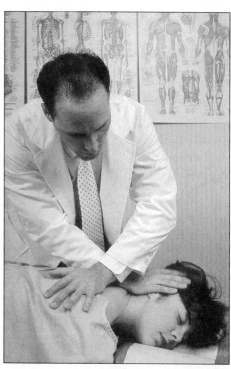

2.

3.

4.

5.

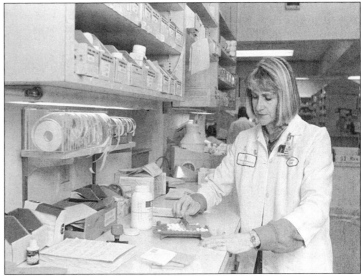

6.

1. What do you think is happening in each picture?

_____

_____

_____

_____

_____

_____

2. How might the healing practice in each picture work?

_____

_____

_____

_____

_____

_____

_____

_____

_____

_____

_____

3. Which of the healing practices in these photos have you experienced? Which are common in your country or culture?

_____

_____

_____

_____

_____

_____

4. What are the advantages and disadvantages of the practices that you are familiar with?

_____

_____

_____

_____

_____

_____

5. What are some other healing practices that are not pictured here?

_____

_____

_____

_____

_____

_____

2   Discuss the following in small groups:

Does culture influence medical care and healing practices? Think about the following cultural aspects of medicine and healing. If possible, give examples of treatments and practices that are influenced by culture.

a. The doctor-patient relationship

b. Whether mind and body are treated separately

c. To what degree the patient is responsible for his or her own healing

d. Whether there are illnesses that are recognized in one culture but not in another

e. Who pays for medical care and medicines

f. Other

Reading for Ideas

3   The following reading selection is titled "The Shaman and the Scientist," by Elizabeth Royte. (A *shaman* is a spiritual person who uses magic to cure the sick.) The article describes how researchers from a small company are searching the globe for medicinal plants. Discuss the following questions in small groups.

Prereading Questions

1. Do you know of any plants that have specific healing effects? What are they?

   _____

   _____

2. In what parts of the world do people practice herbal medicine?

   _____

   _____

The Shaman and the Scientist

The tall, blond scientist makes his way down the forest path, bending over nearly double to get under vines and leafy vegetation. Behind him, a weary M.D. in a polo shirt totes a canvas sack. At the front of this procession is a barefoot curandero, a medicine man, who observes their progress with a bemused air.
5 The Americans are writing down what he says, videotaping the roots he shows them, and tasting the ants from the nodes he claims have therapeutic value. "Interesante," the gringos say, nodding to each other and smiling, their discomfort showing only a little.

Here in the lowland rain forest of Amazonian Ecuador, Steven King, the
10 ethnobotanist, and Tom Carlson, the physician, are looking for medicinal plants—leaves, stems, fruits, and roots that indigenous peoples have used to heal themselves for centuries—for a small pharmaceutical (drug) company. Since arriving in Molino ten days ago in a small prop plane, they've fished in the river, climbed trees without ropes, fired blowgun darts, and butchered a bull that
15 fed the entire village during their stay.

They've also collected thirty-five pounds of plants. Their guide, Elias, is a Quichua Indian who wears a jag-uar tooth around his neck and a
20 machete across his chest. During their trek, King shows Elias photo-graphs of various skin conditions—a lesion, a fungal infection, a rash. The shaman considers the photos and,
25 more often than not, leads King to plants he believes may help. "Here," he says, pointing with his machete. "Look at this *chuchu huasi*," or *supa y chacra* or *pajopanga*. If all goes
30 well, this man will help the pharma-ceutical company develop new, low-cost drugs that could treat millions—and help save the rain for-est at the same time.

35   People have been using plants to treat illness since before history was recorded. Four thousand years ago, the Red Emperor of China published a compendium of some four hundred medicinal plants in common use. Today, 80 percent of the Third World relies on plant-derived medicine for its primary health care. In the First World, a full quarter of our prescription drugs are obtained from
40 plants. Among the best known are quinine, which comes from the Peruvian cinchona tree and is used to treat malaria; morphine, an analgesic and sedative, from poppies; the cardiac stimulant digitalis, from foxglove; and the muscle relaxant curare, which the Makushi Indians of Guyana used as a poison on their spear tips. Certainly the star among higher medicinal plants is the rosy peri-
45 winkle, from which Eli Lilly and Company makes two cancer-fighting drugs.

    For over two hundred other companies worldwide looking for medicine in natural products, it's a race to find these plants before they disappear with the tropical rain forests. It's also a race for profits: Medicinal plants currently bring the pharmaceutical industry about $12 billion a year. But that's just the tip of the
50 iceberg. Fewer than 1 percent of the 250,000 known plant species have been tested thoroughly for medicinal properties.

    Tropical rain forests contain 70 percent of the world's plant species, but in the last four decades, nearly half have been lost. Every minute, close to a hun-dred acres of forest fall to the logger's saw or the farmer's torch. At this rate, the
55 rain forests will be destroyed in a matter of decades. When the forest goes, so will a vast chemical repository of plants and animals, as well as the people who know how to use them. Every day, a hundred rain forest species die, species that may not yet be described, species that could one day yield cures for dis-eases yet to be recognized.

Postreading Questions

4   Answer these questions.

1. What are the Americans doing at the beginning of the article? Where are they and why are they there? Why might they feel "a little" uncomfortable?

_____

_____

_____

_____

_____

2. Which of the healing plants that are mentioned in the article are you familiar with? Have you been treated with any of these?

_____

_____

_____

_____

_____

3. What are the two "races" Royte describes?

_____

_____

_____

_____

_____

Thinking Critically

Making Predictions

Practice making predictions. Work in small groups and answer the following questions based on the information in the article "The Shaman and the Scientist" and your own knowledge:

■   What is your prediction for the future of medicinal plants?

■   Will work in the rain forest continue and increase, or will it become impossible?

Freewriting

5   Are herbal medicines effective, in your opinion? Write on this topic for twenty minutes without stopping. Support your point of view by relating any experiences you may have had with herbal remedies.

Gathering Information

6   Do research on a healing practice that is new to you. Find out what the treatment involves, how it affects the patient, with which group of people or in what part of the world it has been used, and how effective the treatment is. You may wish to choose one of the following topics or another one:

- hypnotism
- psychotherapy
- homeopathy
- chiropractic medicine

- herbal medicine
- acupuncture
- nutrition therapy

You may do Web or library research on the practice you have chosen, interview someone who has undergone the treatment, or a combination.

7   Form groups of three or four with students who have investigated a healing practice different from the one you did research on in Activity 6. Then read the descriptions of the following people and their illnesses. As a group, choose four patients. Discuss how a practitioner of the therapy you did research on would treat each patient. Discuss also the cross-cultural differences, if any, in the treatment of the illness. Note the similarities and differences among the various approaches.

> **Patient A** is an eight-year-old boy with a persistent stomachache. He has had it for one week and during this time has been unable to go to school or engage in any other activities.
>
> **Patient B** is a thirty-two-year-old woman. She feels tired all the time and does not have enough energy to engage in her everyday activities. She has felt this way for the last two weeks.
>
> **Patient C** is a fifty-five-year-old man with high blood pressure. He does not have any physical discomfort because of it, but his doctor tells him it is way above the normal range.
>
> **Patient D** is a twenty-five-year-old woman with a pain in her neck. It is painful for her to turn her head from side to side, and she is very uncomfortable lying in bed.
>
> **Patient E** is a one-year-old boy who has been diagnosed as anemic. His parents were told that he does not eat enough food with iron in it. The child has no symptoms.
>
> **Patient F** is a sixty-five-year-old woman who has no desire to eat. She began to lose her appetite about a week ago and has had very little solid food since then. She is now losing weight rapidly and is weak.

Patient G is a twenty-nine-year-old man with a persistent backache. He cannot identify any incident or accident that may have caused it, although the pain began about two days after his wife gave birth to their first child.

Patient H is a nineteen-year-old woman who is twenty pounds overweight. She leads a fairly active life and claims that she has been dieting for the last two months, but she has lost no weight. Her condition is causing no health problems, but she would like to weigh less.

<table>
<tr><td>PART 2</td></tr>
</table>

Language for Writing

Understanding Prefixes and Suffixes in Medical Terminology

1 Look at the medical terms in the following chart. Note what part of speech each is. Make sure you know what it means. Then, with a partner, think of as many different forms of each word as you can and fill in the blank spaces in the chart. The spaces indicate the most common forms of these terms; you may think of more. Make sure that the new word forms relate to the topic of medicine.

Note that (1) there are different noun forms for people and things for some of the terms, and (2) there may be more than one word for a particular category. If so, explain the difference between the words. For example, *medication* is a drug; *medicine* refers to drugs in general or a field of study or practice.

Nouns		Verbs	Adjectives	Adverbs
Person	**Thing**			
medic	medication		_____	_____
	medicine		_____	medicinally
_____	_____		therapeutic	_____
_____	healing	_____	healing	
herbalist	_____		_____	
	diagnosis	_____	_____	
	_____	treat	treatable	
practitioner	_____	_____		
_____	pharmacy			
_____	_____		psychological	_____
_____	_____		biological	

2   Answer these questions about the word forms in the chart in Activity 1. Use a dictionary if necessary.

1. What is the difference between *medicinal* and *medical*?

_____

_____

2. What is a *diagnosis*? How is it different from a *treatment*?

_____

_____

3. What do you call the practitioners of the following?

    a. therapy
    b. herbalism
    c. pharmacology
    d. psychology
    e. biology

   What ending do all the terms for the practitioner have in common? List some other fields in which the word for the practitioner has the same word ending.

_____

_____

_____

_____

4. Which term is the same for both the adjective and noun forms? Can you think of any other nouns and adjectives that have the same form?

_____

_____

_____

_____

3   Rewrite your Freewriting assignment. This time, use some of the terms in the chart on page 191. Then exchange your Freewriting with a partner and check each other's use of the terms.

4   Choose three of the patients described in Activity 7, pages 190–191. Write a short paragraph for each patient. In the paragraph, give advice based on the information in the chapter, your research, and any other knowledge about medicine you possess. In each paragraph, use various forms of the medical terms from the chart wherever appropriate.

Reviewing Transitions

In this section, you will review transitional expressions that highlight similarities and differences between ideas; in Part 3 you will review ways to organize entire essays that discuss similarities and differences.

Look at the following chart. Notice that there are three types of transitions that you can use to point out similarities and differences.

	1	2	3
Differences		Whereas While Although Even though	However, On the other hand, Conversely,
Similarities	Both . . . and Neither . . . nor		Similarly, Likewise, In the same way,

The first type of transition (column 1) emphasizes similarities between two subjects and uses an affirmative verb.

Examples

Both herbalists **and** fetish priests practice medicine in many parts of Africa.

Neither conventional **nor** alternative approaches to healing have led to a cure for cancer.

The second type of transition (column 2) begins with a dependent clause and is followed by an independent clause.

Examples

Although herbal medicine is not popular in the United States, it is regarded as highly effective in some Asian countries.

While homeopathy is just becoming known in North America, it has been widely used in Europe for many years.

The third type of transition (column 3) links ideas between sentences. These connectors usually appear at the beginning of a sentence and are followed by commas.

Example

In the past, preventative approaches to illness were not strongly emphasized in the education of American doctors. **On the other hand,** preventing rather than curing illness has always been strongly emphasized in European medicine.

Practice using different types of transitions in your writing. Varying your sentences will make your writing livelier and more interesting.

5 Choose one of the patients described in Activity 7, pages 190–191. Write about two different approaches to solving the problem. Use the transition expressions from the second chart in this section.

6 Look at the pictures on pages 184–185. Choose at least two of them and compare the approaches to healing represented in the pictures.

PART 3

Systems for Writing

Comparisons

Review Points
- The way you organize an essay depends on the topic of the essay.
- It's important to keep your reader in mind when you plan essay organization and development.

New Points
- A comparison is a discussion of the similarities or differences (or both) between two or more things.
- You can make comparisons in an entire essay, or in a single paragraph within an essay.
- In a comparison essay, you help the reader by using transitions that show comparison and by developing your ideas fully.
- You also help your reader by expressing all the elements of your comparison in your thesis statement.

1   Study this example of a comparison thesis statement:

Example A

In the United States, herbal medicine is often regarded as ineffective, whereas in some European countries, herbal medicine is highly regarded as an alternative to pharmaceuticals.

The *comparison* is how herbal medicine is regarded in the United States and in Europe. The word that indicates the writer is emphasizing differences rather than similarities is *whereas*.

Now read this thesis statement, which also makes a comparison, and answer the questions that follow:

Example B

Both Nepal and the People's Republic of China devote a great deal of effort to the research and development of herbal remedies.

- ■ Does this thesis emphasize a similarity or a difference?
- ■ How do you know?
- ■ In this thesis statement, what is the thing being compared?
- ■ What is the point of similarity?

(The thing being compared in the preceding thesis statement is herbal remedies. The point of similarity is the research and development of herbal remedies. The comparison word that lets you know the emphasis immediately is *both*.)

2 Look again at the thesis statement in Example A. After you read this statement, how do you expect the essay to be organized? What information do you want to have on the topic?

One pattern to follow in organizing a comparison essay is the following:

I. Introduction

II. All about X

III. All about Y

IV. Conclusion

The thesis statements in Examples A and B prepare the reader for the preceding pattern of organization. Here is how the two essays would look:

A

I. Introduction

II. The role of herbal medicine in the United States

III. The role of herbal medicine in Europe

IV. Conclusion

B

I. Introduction

II. Research of herbal remedies in Nepal

III. Research of herbal remedies in China

IV. Conclusion

3   The organization of these comparisons is simple. However, now look at the following thesis statement, and answer the questions that follow:

Example C

As surprising as it may seem, Western psychotherapists and African healers are very similar in terms of their relationships with their patients and their treatment techniques.

- What is being compared in this thesis statement?
- What is (are) the point(s) of comparison?
- Is the writer emphasizing similarities or differences? What word tells you this?

The thesis statement in Example C has another common pattern of comparison organization:

   I.   Introduction (X & Y)

   II.   One point of comparison

        Examples from X in relation to this point

        Examples from Y in relation to this point

   III.   Another point of comparison

        Examples from X in relation to the second point

        Examples from Y in relation to the second point

   IV.   Conclusion

Here's a diagram of how the essay comparing Western psychotherapists and African healers would look:

   I.   Introduction (Western psychotherapists & African healers)

   II.   Patient relationship

        African examples

        Western examples

   III.   Treatment techniques

        African examples

        Western examples

   IV.   Conclusion

Note that this pattern of organization is a little more complex than the other one; it requires the use of more transitions to coordinate the ideas so that the reader can follow them easily.

Most comparisons can be organized either way; the choice depends on how complex your focus on the topic is and on what you want to emphasize.

Focus on Testing

Getting Your Thesis Right

The example thesis statements on pages 194–196 show you how a well-written thesis statement acts as a plan for a well-written essay. In test-taking situations, remember to get your thesis right before you start. Think of it as an outline for your essay and you'll produce good work more quickly and easily.

4 Compare the following items by emphasizing similarities or differences as indicated. First, brainstorm by yourself for ideas on each topic, then write a thesis statement and an outline of an organizational pattern. When you have finished, show your ideas to a partner. Compare your organizational patterns and discuss the reasons for your choices, especially where your approaches are different.

1. your native language / English (differences)
2. learning a foreign language in the classroom / learning a foreign language outside the classroom (differences)
3. space exploration / undersea exploration (similarities)
4. women's speech / men's speech (differences)
5. adolescence in one culture / in your culture (similarities)
6. doing business in the United States or Canada / doing business in your culture (differences)
7. your definition of social responsibility / someone else's definition (differences)
8. the work of one artist / the work of another artist (similarities)

Writing Assignments

Write an essay on one of the following topics. Use the ideas you've discussed and written about so far in this chapter as the basis for your essay.

1. Compare an aspect of healing in two cultures. Possible points of comparison might be
   a. doctor-patient relationship
   b. treatments
   c. whether mind and body are treated separately
   d. patient responsibility in the healing process
   e. an illness that exists in one culture but not in another
   f. who pays for medical care and medicines

2. Compare different attitudes toward medicine or healing or both within one culture. For example, you could compare traditional healing to modern, Western medicine.

3. Choose a method of healing. Compare it with other healing methods in the introduction as a way to get started. Remember to focus on one important point in the thesis.

4. Discuss the role of doctors in medicine today. Do they have a responsibility to treat their patients or educate their patients or both? Discuss this question with your teacher and classmates to help you gather information and generate vocabulary before you get started.

5. Write about any aspect of medicine that interests you.

PART 4   Evaluating for Rewriting

Evaluating the First Draft

Step 1

Choose a partner and exchange your essays. Read your partner's first draft to get the general idea; don't focus on specific details or on grammar or punctuation. Use the following questions to evaluate each other's essays.

1. What is the main idea?

   _____

   _____

2. What is the writer's purpose in writing this essay?

   _____

   _____

3. Did the writer accomplish what he or she set out to do?

   Yes _____   No _____

4. Do you have any suggestions for improving this first draft?

   _____

   _____

Step 2

Return each other's essays. Read your partner's evaluation. Discuss any questions you have with your partner.

Step 3

Now write a second draft, considering your partner's evaluation comments.

Evaluating the Second Draft

Step 1

Exchange your second drafts. Use the following questions to evaluate your partner's essay.

1. Write your partner's thesis statement:

   _____

   _____

   _____

   _____

   Does it emphasize similarities or differences?

   _____

   _____

   _____

   How do you know? Write the word(s) or expression(s) that tell(s) you:

   _____

   _____

   _____

2. What pattern of organization do you expect the writer to follow?

   _____

   _____

   _____

3. What do you expect this essay to be about?

   _____

   _____

   _____

4. Now read the rest of the essay. Was your guess about the organizational pattern correct?

   Yes _____   No _____

   If not, make suggestions for improvement.

   _____

   _____

   _____

5. Were your other expectations met?

Yes _____   No _____

If not, make suggestions for improvement.

_____

_____

_____

6. Did the writer use words and expressions from Part 2, Language for Writing, in this essay? Give some examples:

_____

_____

_____

7. Did the writer use them correctly?

Yes _____   No _____

8. Do you have any suggestions for the writer in future work?

_____

_____

_____

9. What did you particularly like about this essay?

_____

_____

_____

Step 2

Return your second drafts. Read your partner's evaluation. Discuss any questions you have with your partner.

Writing the Final Draft

Now write a final draft, considering your partner's comments. Turn in this draft to your teacher.

Video Activities: Stealth Surgery

Before You Watch.   Answer these questions in small groups.

1. What kinds of pictures does an X-ray machine take? Have you ever had an X-ray?

2. Do you know the name of any other machines that can take pictures of the inside of a body? What are they? How are they different from X-rays?

Watch.   Answer these questions in small groups.

1. What is Leonard Novak's favorite free time activity? Why is it unusual?

   _____

   _____

2. What health problem did Leonard Novak have recently?

   a. eye problems   b. bad headaches   c. a cancerous tumor

3. What is the name of the new treatment that Novak received?

   _____

4. Why is this treatment better than traditional surgery?

   _____

   _____

Watch Again.   Answer these questions in small groups.

1. Use the words below to complete the description of the new treatment.

anatomical	converted	creates	CT
images	MRI	placed	scans

   Two hundred or more _____ and _____ _____
   of the patient's head are fed into the computer and _____ into 3D
   _____. Then a band _____ on the patient's head
   _____ an _____ map.

2. *He was benched* means that he _____.

   a. couldn't play

   b. was hit with a bench

   c. got sick

3. *She threw him a curve ball* means that she _____.

   a. hit him

   b. pitched the ball to him

   c. surprised him

4. The word *invasive* is an adjective related to _____.

   a. invalid   b. invasion   c. invent

5. The *skull* is the _____.

   a. bone of the head   b. the nose   c. the neck bone

6. *Stealth* refers to the action of moving _____.

   a. quickly   b. secretly   c. carefully

After You Watch.   Procedures such as Leonard Novak's are extremely expensive. Should society be trying to perfect treatments such as these or should it spend money improving basic health care for all? Write an essay giving your opinion on this question.

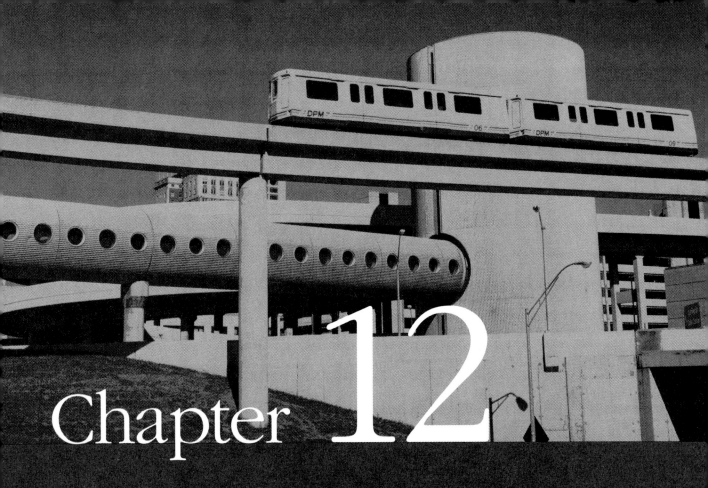

Chapter 12

The Future

PART 1	# Ideas for Writing

Getting Started

We are at the beginning of a new century. What will this century bring?

1   Look at these photos of recent developments. Then answer the questions that follow.

1. Development in technology

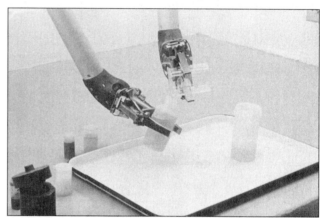

2. Robot arms at work

3. Easier, faster communication

4. This spacecraft will observe the Sun's surface and the solar wind.

5. Electric-powered: Car of the future?

6. Living longer vigorous lives

1. How have personal computers and the Internet changed the average person's life in recent years? How will they continue to change our lives in the future?

_____

_____

_____

2. In the future, will robots replace humans in some jobs? Give examples.

_____

_____

_____

3. How have cell phones revolutionized communication for individuals and industry?

_____

_____

_____

4. Should we continue to explore space? Is it more important than spending money to decrease world hunger and the diminishing ozone layer?

_____

_____

_____

5. What are the advantages and disadvantages of using alternative energy sources on a large scale? Will electric cars become more popular?

_____

_____

_____

6. As people are living longer, what changes do you predict?

_____

_____

_____

7. Write your own question about the future:

_____

_____

_____

2 In small groups, discuss one of the following topics. Consider the impact your topic will have on some of the following areas: jobs, health and longevity, interpersonal relationships, and international relations.

Topics
- e-commerce
- robotics
- communication innovations
- space exploration
- alternative energy sources
- geriatrics (study of physical processes and problems of aging)

Reading for Ideas

3 The following reading is from an interview that asked people to talk about what they predicted would be the most important issues of the twenty-first century. Before you read, answer these questions:

Prereading Questions

1. What do you think were the three most important changes that took place in the twenty-first century?

_____

_____

_____

2. What are three important changes that you think the twenty-first century will bring?

_____

_____

_____

What Will Be the Top Stories of the Twenty-First Century?

From *USA Weekend*

Technology will transform our lives

"Life spans will extend 100 to 150 years, and
5 childbirth at 50 and 60 will be common. Many will have three or four careers as well as at least one chapter as full-
10 time parent and another as philanthropist."

—Candice Carpenter, co-founder and CEO, iVillage.com

The United States will have a new face

"Hispanics, Asians, Pacific Islanders, African Americans and European
15 immigrants (e.g., Armenians) will alter the classic 'American character' and give the USA a new type of American."

—Fernando M. Torres-Gil, Associate Dean and Professor, UCLA School of Public Policy

Medicine will create moral dilemmas

20 "The big stories of the 21st century will have nothing to do with politics and everything to do with the changes in health and technology and the moral decision humans will be **confronted with** having to do with life and death."

—Cokie Roberts, ABC News Correspondent and *USA Weekend* Contributing Editor

25 *The divorce rate will drop*

"By adjusting our expectations of the opposite sex, men and women will achieve greater **intimacy** and happiness, thus strengthening the family unit."

—John Gray, author of *Men Are From Mars, Women Are From Venus*

30 *The first black President will be elected*

"In the past 100 years, African Americans have **made tremendous strides** to become full partners in society. It's just a question of the right person running for office."

—Robert Johnson, Founder and President, Black
35 Entertainment Television

Programs for old will threaten the economy

"As more than 70 million **baby boomers become eligible for** Social Security and Medicare, these programs will run operating **deficits** in the trillions of dollars, **imperiling** the entire economy."

40 —Richard Thau, President, Generation X Think Tank Third Millennium

Postreading Questions

4   Answer these questions.

1. Write each prediction in your own words then indicate the field it applies to on the following chart. An example is provided.

Prediction	Technology	Demographics (Human populations)	Human Relationships	Geriatrics
People will live twice as long as they live now.	✔			

2. Which prediction do you most strongly agree with?

_____

_____

_____

Thinking Critically

Considering Alternative Opinions

Making predictions about the future often involves stating strong opinions. There can be opposing points of view. When a writer tries to convince you to believe something about the future or about any controversial issue, try to think of arguments that would support a different, or opposing opinion. This will increase your objectivity and it will clarify your own opinion. Practice by jotting down opposing points of view for the following issues:

1. The beautification and preservation of the environment needs to be the first priority in this new century.

    _____

2. Cultural differences between people will cause more conflicts as communication makes the world smaller.

    _____

3. Finding a cure for AIDS is the single most important issue in our world.

    _____

4. The "information age" will continue to alienate people from each other and create medical and psychological problems.

    _____

Freewriting

5   The article you read describes some predictions for the future. Describe your own impression of what life will be like as this century progresses. Will life be easier or more difficult? Will the problems of today be solved or become worse? What new problems will we have? What advantages or benefits will the future bring? Write for twenty minutes without stopping.

Gathering Information

6   Find out more about one of the aspects of the future shown at the beginning of this chapter or discussed in the reading. As you do your research, focus on the subject's positive and negative effects on the community, the environment, the economy, and human behavior and attitudes. You may wish to choose one of the following:

- computers
- communication technology
- robotics
- alternative energy research

- space exploration
- changing family and sex roles
- use of natural resources
- demographics

Take notes on the chart provided.

	Community	Environment	Economy	Behavior, Attitudes
Positive Effects				
Negative Effects				

7   You are going to hold a debate with your classmates. You will argue for or against the further development of current research or a current social trend. Follow these steps:

1. Think of some current trends that seem to be setting the foundation for the future, such as those in the pictures at the beginning of the chapter. Here are some ideas:
   - computers in education
   - genetic engineering
   - use of robots in factories
   - computers that reason like humans ("artificial intelligence")
   - space exploration
   - changing family and sex roles
   - use of natural resources
   - the effect(s) of changing demographics

2. After you have chosen a topic, develop a statement, or *resolution,* that says whether you think the outcomes of the trend will be positive or negative.

3. Divide into teams and develop the arguments for your side. The information you collected in the Gathering Information section will be useful here. Develop at least three major arguments for your side, and prepare at least three arguments to counter what you predict the other side will say. See Chapter 8, page 142, for information on how to conduct a debate.

PART 2	# Language for Writing

Using Computer Terminology

1 Review some common terms associated with the parts and operation of a personal computer. Divide into teams of two or three. Try to be the first group in your class to find the correct meanings for the terms in the list. To win, your definitions or explanations *must* be in nontechnical language. The team that also draws or finds pictures of the items gets extra points. (*Hint:* Look for advertisements for computer products in magazines and newspapers.)

hub	E-mail	software	word processing
database	spreadsheet	hardware	computer language
cross platform	keyboard	desktop publishing	DSL
integrated	monitor (video display)	terminal (VDT)	
LCD player	floppy disk	disk drive	
server	hard disk	modem	

Making Qualified Predictions

When writers predict the future, they use certain words and structures to *qualify* their statements. No one knows *exactly* what the future holds so writers must limit what they say. Some reporters qualify their ideas about the future by using the modal *could:*

> If these conditions continue, there *could be* a more serious problem in the future.

In this case, he uses *could* + verb to express a *possibility* about the future.

Another way to make qualified predictions about the future is with the use of the modal *would* + verb to express outcomes dependent upon a condition expressed in an *if* clause. Study this example:

> If everyone worked from home computers, there *would be* many changes in our social structure.

Note the form of the verb in the *if* clause.

Sometimes we use *would* + verb without the *if* clause when the condition is *understood*. For example, a statement following the one you just saw might be:

> People *would save* energy and time by not having to commute to an office every day.

(What is the understood condition?)

What modal do we use to express *certainty* about the future? Read the following sentence:

> More people *will have* home computers in the future.

2   Make predictions about your future using *could* + verb, *if. . . , would* + verb, and *will* + verb, depending on how certain you are and whether there are any conditions to be met. You might answer the following questions: Where will you be in the year 2020? What will you be doing? Who will you be with?

3   Read the following newspaper article about the predictions of a futurist who is very certain about what work will be like in the year 2020. You are not so sure. Rewrite his ideas, qualifying the predictions by replacing each instance of the modal *will*.

The world of work is changing, fundamentally and decisively, according to futurist Daniel Bell, a professor of social sciences at Harvard University.

In the new society, "work will be a game between people," according to Bell. This contrasts with the nature of work in the factory-centered industrial society, which he called "a game against manufactured nature and the machine," and that of preindustrial work such as agriculture, "a game against nature."

"[The] nine-to-five [work day] will be obsolete," he says. "Work hours will be staggered, individualized; more facilities will be used twenty-four hours a day. The computer revolution will enable people to conduct their business at home, at the beach, wherever they choose."

---

4   Read what you wrote for the Freewriting assignment. How certain were you of what you wrote? Rewrite the assignment, using the modals presented in this section to indicate a greater or lesser degree of certainty.

5   Write a paragraph in which you predict the role computers will play in your community in the year 2025. Include words and expressions from this section.

PART 3   # Systems for Writing

Summarizing

Review Point

■   In a comparison essay, you choose an organization pattern that highlights the point you want to emphasize.

New Points

- A summary is a report on something that has already been written or presented orally.
- It is shorter than the original, but it contains all the important points. Minor points—such as details, facts, and examples used to illustrate the main ideas in the original—are omitted.
- The first sentence of a summary usually identifies what is being summarized: the author, title, and/or source and includes the main ideas of the original.
- The ideas in a summary should be in the same order as they are in the original.
- Summaries are usually written in the present tense.
- The writer of the summary should not express personal opinions about the material being summarized. The only opinions in the summary should be those of the original author.

1   Read the following summary of the interview on future predictions. Then answer the questions that follow.

In "What Will Be the Top Stories of the Twenty-First Century?," six prominent professionals make predictions about how life will be different in the next century. The predictions are that technology will transform our lives, that the classic American character will change as minority groups grow, that developments in medicine will create moral dilemmas, that there will be fewer divorces, that Americans will elect an African American president, and finally, that the large numbers of senior citizens will be a drain on the economy.

1. How long is the original article? How long is the summary?

2. What is the purpose of the first sentence in the summary? What information does it contain?

3. Look at the original article again. How many main ideas are there? What are they? Now look at the summary. Are the same ideas discussed? Are any missing?

4. Notice the order of ideas in the original. Is the same order used in the summary?

    _____

    _____

5. Notice the use of details, facts, and illustrations in the original article. Do many of these details appear in the summary? Why not?

    _____

    _____

6. Whose ideas are expressed in the summary? How do you know? Do any opinions appear in the summary that are not in the original article? Why or why not?

    _____

    _____

7. What tenses are used in the original article? What tenses are used in the summary?

    _____

    _____

Whenever you are asked to write an essay in which you react to something you've read, the introduction of your essay can become a summary that leads into your thesis statement (see Chapter 9, Part 3). The pattern of organization for an essay that consists of a summary and reaction looks like this:

Paragraph 1:	Summary of reading
	Last sentence: your thesis (that is, your opinion of what the author has said)
Paragraph 2:	Body
Paragraph 3:	Body
Last Paragraph:	Conclusion

Focus on Testing

Mastering the Art of Summary Writing

Because many essay tests require that you respond to a reading selection, it is important to be able to restate the main ideas of this selection quickly and easily. Review the tips for writing a good summary until you have mastered them. This will give you an advantage when you are writing under time pressure.

2 Summarize the following reading selections from this book. For each one, keep in mind the guidelines for writing a summary outlined in this section. Each summary should be about one paragraph in length.

1. "Want to Learn a Language? Don't Make It a Mount Everest" in Chapter 1 on pages 5–6.
2. "Annapurna: A Woman's Place" in Chapter 2 on pages 26–27.
3. "Gender Differences in Communication" in Chapter 3 on page 46.
4. "Rites of Passage in American Society" in Chapter 5 on pages 83–85.
5. "Decision by Consensus" in Chapter 7 on pages 121–122.

Writing Assignments

Write an essay on at least one of the following topics. Use the ideas you've discussed and the material you've written so far in this chapter and previous chapters as the basis for your essay.

1. Discuss the possible negative or positive effects of an aspect of the future you did research on in this chapter. Consider community, environmental, economic, and psychological effects.
2. Write an essay on the argument your side presented in the debate from this chapter (Part 1). Consider the four areas of impact.
3. Write an essay about a development in one of the fields mentioned in this chapter.
4. Write an essay on any aspect of the future that interests you.

| PART 4 | # Evaluating for Rewriting |

Evaluating the First Draft

Step 1

Choose a partner and exchange your essays. Read your partner's first draft to get the general idea; don't focus on specific details or on grammar or punctuation. Use the following questions to evaluate each other's essays.

1. What is the main idea?

_____

_____

2. What is the writer's purpose in writing this essay?

_____

_____

3. Did the writer accomplish what he or she set out to do?

    Yes _____   No _____

4. Do you have any suggestions for improving the first draft?

    _____

    _____

Step 2

Return each other's essays. Read your partner's evaluation. Discuss any questions you have with your partner.

Step 3

Now write a second draft, considering your partner's evaluation comments.

Evaluating the Second Draft

For the second draft of the essay, devise your own evaluation questionnaire. Work with a partner and develop your questions, keeping in mind all the important points you've learned about essay writing since the beginning of this course. You may wish to skim through the Systems for Writing section (Part 3) of each chapter and the evaluation questionnaires appearing at the end of each chapter. Make sure you include questions on essay form, the thesis sentence, the development and organization of ideas, summarizing, and introductions and conclusions. Write your questions in the following spaces, then exchange essays and use your questionnaire to evaluate your partner's essay.

1. _____
2. _____
3. _____
4. _____
5. _____
6. _____
7. _____
8. _____
9. _____
10. _____

Writing the Final Draft

Now write a final draft, considering your partner's comments. Turn in this draft to your teacher.

Video Activities: Concept Cars

Before You Watch.   Answer these questions in small groups.

1. What does the word *concept* mean?

    a. beginning   b. idea   c. imagination

2. Describe the kind of car that you would like to own. You can describe one that exists or use your imagination.

Watch.   Answer these questions in small groups.

1. Which of these statements is true?

    a. All concept cars become production cars.

    b. Car manufacturers use concept cars to "try out" new ideas.

    c. Concept cars are too expensive to build.

2. Which of these concept cars did not become production cars?

    a. the Avalanche   c. the PT Cruiser

    b. the Lacrosse   d. the Prowler

3. Write the name of the concept car next to the correct description.

    a. video monitors and voice-activated   _____
        lights and turn signals

    b. a popular design   _____

    c. a combination of a truck
        and an SUV   _____

Watch Again.   Circle the correct answers.

1. Which of these car companies are mentioned in the video segment?

    a. Ford   c. Chrysler-Daimler   e. Toyota
    b. Mercedes   d. Chevrolet (Chevy)   f. Buick

2. It's a real *eye-popper* means it looks _____.

    a. great   b. dangerous   c. terrible

3. *I'm a Ford man* means _____.

    a. He works for Ford.

    b. He buys Ford cars.

    c. His name is Ford.

4. "The club *just got its motor running* last December" means that it just
_____.

a. bought a car   b. fixed an engine   c. started

After You Watch.   Write a description of a car that you would like to own or one that you think would be good for society (environmentally friendly for example). Be as detailed as you can and feel free to imagine things that are not yet possible.

Text Credits

Pages 5–6 "Want to Learn a Language? Don't Make It a Mount Everest" by Tish Durkin, *New York Times,* September 26, 1992, copyright 1992 by The New York Times Company. Adapted by permission; *pages 26–27* "Annapurna: A Woman's Place" by Arlene Blum. Copyright 1980 by Arlene Blum. Adapted by permission of Sierra Club Books; *page 46* "Gender Differences in Communication" by Rose Der at http://www.geocities.com/Wellesley/2052/genddiff.html. Copyright 1997–2000 by Rose Ker. Adapted by permission; *pages 62–63* "The Giza Pyramids" from *Egypt.* Reprinted by permission of Editions Marcus, Paris; *pages 83–85* "Rites of Passage in American Society" from *Sociology,* Fourth Edition, by Richard T. Schaefer and Robert P. Lamm. McGraw-Hill, Inc., New York, 1992. Adapted by permission; *pages 100–102* "Decision by Consensus" from *The Rising Sun on Main Street, Working with the Japanese, 2e* by Alison R. Lanier, International Information Associates, Inc., Yardley, 1992. Adapted by permission; *pages 156–157* "African Art as Nonverbal Communication" from *Contemporary Arts and Crafts* by Thelma R. Newman, copyright 1974 by Thelma R. Newman. Adapted by permission of Crown Publishers, Inc.; *pages 172–173* Selections from *Turtle Island.* Copyright 1974 by Gary Snyder. Reprinted by permission of New Directions Publishing Corp.; *pages 187–188* Excerpt from "The Shaman and the Scientist" by Elizabeth Royte from *San Francisco Focus Magazine,* Vol. 40, No. 3, August 1993. Reprinted by permission; *page 207* "What Will Be the Top Stories of the 21st Century?" by Evelyn Poitevent from *USA Weekend,* Dec. 24–26, 1999. Adapted by permission.

Photo Credits

Chapter 1 Opener ©James Marshall/The Image Works; *page 2 (top left)* ©Todd Gipstein/CORBIS, *(top right)* ©Peter Menzel, *(bottom left)* ©Burbank/The Image Works, *(bottom right)* ©David Young-Wolff/PhotoEdit; *page 5* ©Peter Menzel/Stock, Boston; *Chapter 2 Opener* ©Hulton-Deutsch Collection/CORBIS; *page 22 (top left)* ©Bettmann/CORBIS, *(top middle)* ©Bettmann/CORBIS, *(top right)* Marin County Historical Society, *(bottom left)* Mary Evans Picture Library/Photo Researchers, *(bottom right)* ©Hulton Getty/Archive Photos; *page 23 (top left)* ©UPI/Bettmann/ CORBIS, *(top right)* ©UPI/Bettmann/CORBIS, *(middle left)* ©Bettmann/CORBIS, *(middle right)* Associated Press/Fort Collins Coloradoan, *(bottom left)* ©Michael Lewis/CORBIS; *page 26* ©Galen Rowell/CORBIS; *Chapter 3 Opener* ©Richard Lord/The Image Works; *page 44 (top left and right)* ©Michael Newman/PhotoEdit, *(bottom left and right)* ©John Fung; *page 49* ©Michael Newman/PhotoEdit; *Chapter 4 Opener* ©Rhoda Sidney/PhotoEdit; *page 60 (top left)* ©Dave G. Houser/CORBIS, *(top right)* Comstock, *(middle left)* ©Buddy Mays/CORBIS, *(middle right)* ©Stock, Boston, *(bottom left)* Lucas/The Image Works; *Chapter 5 Opener* ©John Coletti/ Stock, Boston; *page 80 (top left)* ©F. J. Dean/The Image Works, *(top right)* ©Jose Carrillo/PhotoEdit, *(bottom left)* ©Cassy M. Cohen/PhotoEdit, *(bottom right)* ©Bonnie Kamin/PhotoEdit; *page 81 (top left)* Tom McCarthy/PhotoEdit, *(top right)*